BARNES & NOBLE
COMPLETE
ILLUSTRATED MAP
AND GUIDEBOOK TO

CENTRAL PARK

Concept, Design, Maps and Photographs by
Richard J. Berenson

Text by Raymond Carroll

Produced for
Silver Lining Books
New York
by
Berenson Design & Books, Ltd.
New York

Library of Congress Cataloging-in-Publication Data
is available on request.

ISBN 0-7607-1660-9

10 9 8 7 6 5 4 3 2 1

First Edition

Additional Credits:

Cover photograph © 1999 Ned B. Wood

© 1999 Julian Olivas/Air-to-Ground: *22-23 top left*

Art Institute of Chicago: *8-9 top*
Maurice Brazil Prendergast, American, 1859-1924,
The Terrace Bridge, Central Park,
watercolor over graphite, on ivory wove paper, 1901, 38.6 x 56.6 cm
The Olivia Shaler Swan Memorial Collection, 1939.431,
photograph © 1999, The Art Institute of Chicago.
All Rights Reserved.

Library of Congress, Washington, DC:
36-37 top, 42-43 top, 60 bottom left

© Hulton-Getty/Liaison Agency: *84*

© The Metropolitan Museum of Art: *82*
Department of Egyptian Art, photo Felix Bonfils, c. 1878

© The Museum of the City of New York: *11, 12, 13, 14-15 top,
48-49, 54 bottom, 73, 89, 100-101, 109*

© Collection of The New-York Historical Society:
*14 bottom, 24-25 top, 25 bottom, 40 top and bottom right,
60-61 bottom, 92 bottom, 106*

Rare Books Division, The New York Public Library,
Astor, Lenox and Tilden Foundations:
8-9 bottom, 10, 19, 36 middle, 44 middle, 63 top right, 71 (detail)

Eno Collection, Miriam and Ira D. Wallach Division of Art,
Prints and Photographs, The New York Public Library,
Astor, Lenox and Tilden Foundations: *60-61 top*

The illustrations appearing on pages 112-115 are reproduced from
BOOK OF NORTH AMERICAN BIRDS,
copyright © 1990 The Reader's Digest Association, Inc.
Used by permission of The Reader's Digest Association, Inc.

This book is dedicated to
Frederick Law Olmsted and Calvert Vaux
for their inspired vision
and to the staff and volunteers
of the
Central Park Conservancy,
The Parks Department,
and the
Urban Park Rangers
for their dedication in
maintaining that dream.

CONTENTS

WALKING TOURS

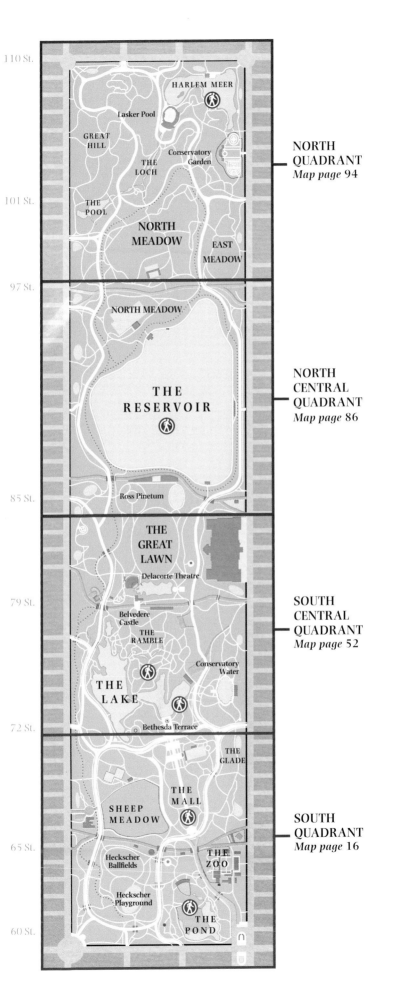

110 St.

HARLEM MEER

Lasker Pool

GREAT HILL

THE LOCH

Conservatory Garden

NORTH QUADRANT
Map page 94

101 St.

THE POOL

NORTH MEADOW

EAST MEADOW

97 St.

NORTH MEADOW

THE RESERVOIR

NORTH CENTRAL QUADRANT
Map page 86

85 St.

Ross Pinetum

THE GREAT LAWN

Delacorte Theatre

79 St.

Belvedere Castle

THE RAMBLE

Conservatory Water

SOUTH CENTRAL QUADRANT
Map page 52

THE LAKE

72 St.

Bethesda Terrace

THE GLADE

THE MALL

SHEEP MEADOW

SOUTH QUADRANT
Map page 16

65 St.

Heckscher Ballfields

THE ZOO

Heckscher Playground

THE POND

60 St.

ENJOYING THE PARK

A visit to Central Park is a pleasant experience. Its scenic grounds have something to interest or delight just about everyone. But newcomers and park aficionados alike occasionally are in need of assistance or information. The following guide explains basic park rules and regulations and offers practical suggestions about park amenities, safety and other concerns.

Rules and Regulations

Park rules require that visitors do not harm the landscape or wildlife. Picking flowers, cutting branches, removing plants, or even digging in park soil are prohibited. Dogs must be leashed and owners must dispose of their dog's waste. Team sports are allowed only in designated areas. Picnicking is both permitted and popular, but camping and barbecuing are prohibited. No commercial activity or amplified sound equipment is allowed without a permit. The park closes at 1 a.m. and opens at dawn. Failure to comply with the rules could result in a summons or arrest.

Finding Your Way

The maps and text in this book will answer most questions about the park. Still, a stop at one or more of its **Visitor Centers** is recommended. They are located in the Dairy, at 65th Street and mid-park; Belvedere Castle, at 79th Street south of the Great Lawn; and the Dana Discovery Center, on the Harlem Meer at 110th Street. Each building is architecturally distinctive, and they are staffed by agreeable volunteers, who can answer your questions or find

the answers. Gifts and park publications are for sale. Central Park information can be reached at (212) 360-3444.

Often after wandering for a while in the park, many people lose track of their whereabouts in relation to the city streets.

The first two numbers embossed on lamppost markers indicate the nearest cross street.

One way of finding out is to examine the lampposts, many of which are numbered. The first two numbers tell which cross street you are near: for example, lampposts numbered 7300 or 7304 are located between 73rd and 74th streets. In the upper park, those numbered 0500 or 0504 are between 105th and 106th streets. Some have the numbers embossed on their dark cast iron surfaces and finding them may take a bit of looking. But more and more lampposts are now sporting easy-to-see, vertical metal strips bearing the instructive numerals.

Safety

Crimes in Central Park make headlines, but it is one of the safest areas in the city. In 1998, only 187 crimes, most of them minor robberies, were reported by the roughly fifteen million people who visited the park. Nevertheless, visitors should exercise common sense by not flashing expensive jewelry or leaving bicycles unguarded. It is never advisable, in fact it is foolish, to roam the park alone after dark, especially in isolated, wooded areas.

In the event of trouble, or if you wish to report a crime, call the **police emergency number: 911**. Police call boxes are scattered throughout the park and their locations are shown on maps in this book. The **Central Park Police** also can be reached at the precinct house on the 85th Street Transverse at mid-park or by calling (212) 570-4820. The **Park Enforcement Patrol (PEP)** enforces park regulations but may also respond to criminal activity. They wear silver and blue badges on their green uniforms and carry batons and mace. They are authorized to issue summonses and make arrests. They can be reached at (212) 427-8700.

Food and Restrooms

Licensed vendors of light food and drink are found in many parts of the park. **The Zoo Cafe** offers reasonably priced fare of the soup-and-sandwich variety in a pleasant, unpretentious setting. Its indoor section is open all year; it also has an attractive outdoor area, but it is open only to zoo patrons and during fair weather.

Far more upscale, the **Tavern on the Green** offers a wide range of contemporary American cuisine at

A favorite spot for children is the Safari Playground located just north of the 90th St. entrance off Central Park West.

lunch and dinner in delightful surroundings. It is open every day of the year at Central Park West and 67th Street. For reservations, call (212) 873-3200. The **Park View Restaurant at the Boathouse** (formerly the Boathouse Cafe) on the northeast corner of the Lake has a charming location and food that has won considerable praise. After 7 p.m., a bus shuttles between Fifth Avenue and 72nd Street and the restaurant. For reservations, call (212) 988-0575.

When weather permits, light fare is offered at the **Ballplayers House** on the north edge of the Heckscher Ballfields and at a pair of kiosks at the park's Columbus Circle entrance.

Public restrooms, as indicated on the maps, are scattered through much of the park. The facilities in the restaurants are better, but usually they are reserved for customers.

Fun for the Kids

The park has an impressive variety of attractions for children. It has twenty-two playgrounds in many sizes and designs, from the sprawling **Heckscher Playground** to the imaginative **Billy Johnson, Safari** and **Ancient playgrounds**. The locations of all are shown on the maps.

Such traditional favorites as the (Wildlife Center) **Zoo**, the **Children's Zoo** and the **Carousel** also retain their charm for the younger set.

The **Swedish Cottage Marionette Theater**, which stages modestly priced marionette performances of classic children's stories such as Goldilocks and the Three Bears, is a special treat for children old enough to sit and pay attention. The theater, a replica of a 19th century Swedish country schoolhouse, is located just southwest of the Delacorte Theater. For information, call (212) 988-9093.

A visit to **Belvedere Castle** is a good option for preteens and teens. The castle and its views of the park are appealing to many kids, and especially interesting to some is its Nature Observatory. It has exhibits on wildlife and a room full of turtle tanks, fossil replicas, plant specimens and useable telescopes and microscopes. For information, call (212) 772-0210.

Wildlife talks and classes for children are also held at the park's **Wildlife Center (Zoo)**. For information, call (212) 439-6518.

A far different attraction is the model boat pond, officially called the **Conservatory Water**. Children not only can watch the boats, they can sail them. Remote-controlled model boats are rented at a stand from 10 a.m. to 7 p.m. Sunday to Friday, and 2 to 7 p.m. on Saturday.

At the north of the pond is the well-known **Alice in Wonderland** statue, a favorite with young children and adults. To the west of the pond, children's stories are told on weekends near the statue of **Hans Christian Andersen**.

ACKNOWLEDGMENTS

Producing this guide required countless days of tramping through the park, documenting its incredible variety, and tapping the extensive knowledge of its zone gardeners and other staff members at the Central Park Conservancy and the Parks Department. The authors wish to thank them for their unstinting assistance.

An array of articles, publications and books were also mined for information. But a special debt is owed to the following works and their authors: *Nature Walks of Central Park* by Dennis Burton; *The Park and the People* by Roy Rosenzweig and Elizabeth Blackmar; *Central Park* by Eugene Kinkead; *Central Park* by Henry Hope Reed and Sophia Duckworth; *Central Park and Prospect Park* by M. M. Graff; *The Central Park Book* by Elizabeth Barlow et al.; and *Country, Park and City* by Francis R. Kowsky.

The Creation of Central Park

Of all New York City's many wonders, Central Park is perhaps the most remarkable. No urban park anywhere can match its combination of inspired landscaping and recreational variety. The green heart of a great city, it has been admired, even cherished, by countless millions of visitors since its birth in the mid-19th century.

How did such a park come to exist in the middle of Manhattan? How was such a marvel of landscape design fashioned on what was once seen as a bleak and uninviting tract of land? Who were the people who created the 843-acre urban oasis?

New York City in the 1840s was growing at a dizzying pace. From a town of roughly 60,000 at the turn of the century, it had become a metropolis of over 312,000. Lamenting the change, writer Washington Irving wrote to his sister in 1847 that "New York, as you knew it, was a mere corner of the present huge city...it is really now one of the most rucketing cities in the world."

In flight from hardships or disasters in Europe, immigrants were flooding into the city. Chiefly Irish and German, many crowded into tenements in lower Manhattan, while even less fortunate ones lived in shanties among the rocks and swamps of the area that was to become Central Park. Malnutrition, disease, contaminated water, and poor sanitation led to an appalling

Irish shanties like these were torn down in the late 1850s to make way for the park. The supervisor's observation tower can be seen at far right.

Bethesda Terrace as interpreted by Maurice Brazil Prendergast in 1901

mortality rate. Polluted air caused by a rapid expansion of industry and commerce in the city was often blamed for the ill health of many city dwellers. In 1844, the editor of the *New York Evening Post*, poet William Cullen Bryant, all but demanded the creation of a large public park. "Commerce is devouring inch by inch the coast of the island," he wrote, "and if we would rescue any part of it for health and recreation it must be done now."

Other voices were also raised. In 1848, Andrew Jackson Downing, America's leading landscape architect and editor of the influential

Horticulturist, called for a huge "People's Park" in the city. A number of publishers and politicians as well as a group of wealthy business-men, some of them idealists, others scenting commercial gain, also joined in the call for a major park.

Mindful of these powerful opinions, in May of 1851 Mayor Ambrose Kingsland made a formal proposal to the city's Common Council that a large public park be built without delay. It met with wide public approval. But where would such a park be located?

For the next two years, the issue was debated in Albany, by the press, and among interested businessmen and landowners. Some preferred a site known as Jones Wood, a hand-some 150-acre property stretching from 66th to 75th streets between Third Avenue and the East River. Downing and a number of politi-cians and civic leaders objected to this, arguing that the present and future needs of the city required a much larger park, more centrally located.

In 1853, a bill passed authorizing the city to purchase the 778 acres bounded by 59th and 106th streets, Fifth Avenue and Eighth Avenue, for the building of "a Central Park."

(The site was extended to 110th Street a decade later, increasing the size to the current 843 acres.)

In 1856, the city took title to the land, and the following year Egbert Viele was named Chief Engineer of the park. The arduous job of clearing the site began, but first the 1,600 or so people who lived on the land had to be dealt with. Squatters, mostly dirt-poor immigrants, resisted attempts by park workers to evict them, and police had to be called in to do the job. Some twenty percent of the park dwellers owned or leased their property. They were compensated and forced to leave; their modest houses, which lined streets just west of today's Great Lawn, were then torn down.

Until 1857, Frederick Law Olmsted had pursued a number of careers with various degrees of success. But that year, in part because his application was supported by Bryant, Irving, and other luminaries such as editor Horace Greeley and botanist Asa Gray, he won the job of Park Superintendent. Under the overall direction of Viele, he was responsible for clearing and construction. Also in charge of the workforce, Olmsted hired craftsmen and laborers on their merits, without regard for their political connections. Writing to his father, he proudly reported "I have got the park into a capital discipline, a perfect system, working like a machine—1000 men now at work."

Calvert Vaux, an English architect, was recruited by Downing and came to the United States in 1850 to work as a partner in the landscaper's Newburgh, New York, office. He built a number of distinctive houses in the area before moving to New York City in 1856 to continue his architectural practice. He also plunged into the ongoing debate over a design for the park.

Judging a design proposed by Chief Engineer Viele to be lacking in imagination, Vaux suggested to the park's Board of Commissioners that a competition be held. When the idea was accepted, Vaux immediately asked Olmsted—whom he had met earlier through Downing—to join with him in preparing a design. After Viele, his park superior, offered no objection, Olmsted agreed to join forces with Vaux. During the winter of 1857-1858, the two men worked

The Men Who Created Central Park. From right to left: Park Superintendent Frederic Law Olmsted, Jacob Wrey Mould, Chief Gardener Ignaz Anton Pilat, Architect Calvert Vaux, George Waring, Jr. and Andrew Haswell Green

Frederick Law Olmsted
Visionary of Central Park

Frederick Law Olmsted was a man who loved parks. Reflecting on his travels in Europe as a young man, the co-designer of Central Park recalled that "While others gravitated to pictures, architecture, Alps, libraries, high life and low life when travelling, I had gravitated to parks—spent all my spare time in them."

Olmsted's passion for parks was to fuel his career as the country's most acclaimed urban landscape architect. Though known chiefly for the green masterpiece in the middle of New York City, he touched places all across Victorian America with his genius.

Olmsted himself said his interest in scenery began at an early age. Born in 1822, the son of a prosperous Hartford, Connecticut, merchant, he had limited formal education, spending more time wandering the woods and fields than with books. Plans to attend Yale were scrapped after a severe reaction to poison sumac, which threatened to damage his eyesight, but young Olmsted was not overly disturbed. "While my mates were fitting for college," he later said, "I was allowed to indulge my strong natural propensity for roaming afield and day-dreaming under a tree."

As a young man, Olmsted failed twice at farming land purchased for him by his father, first in Connecticut and then Staten Island. In 1850, he made a productive six month trip to France, England, Scotland and Ireland, talking with farmers and gardeners, above all visiting public parks and marveling at "the manner in which art had been employed to obtain from nature so much beauty."

On returning home, he wrote *Walks and Talks of an American Farmer in England*, a book that made no profit but gained Olmsted favorable attention. Commissioned by New York's *Daily Times* to travel through the American South, he sent back reports that later were published in three books of critical observations on what he called the Cotton Kingdom. Well received in the North at the time, they are still respected sources on conditions in the pre-Civil War South.

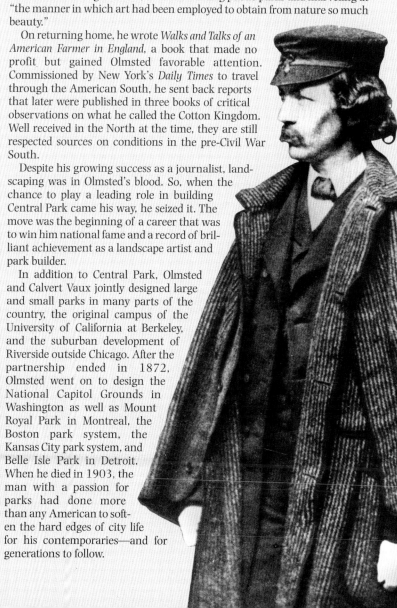

Despite his growing success as a journalist, landscaping was in Olmsted's blood. So, when the chance to play a leading role in building Central Park came his way, he seized it. The move was the beginning of a career that was to win him national fame and a record of brilliant achievement as a landscape artist and park builder.

In addition to Central Park, Olmsted and Calvert Vaux jointly designed large and small parks in many parts of the country, the original campus of the University of California at Berkeley, and the suburban development of Riverside outside Chicago. After the partnership ended in 1872, Olmsted went on to design the National Capitol Grounds in Washington as well as Mount Royal Park in Montreal, the Boston park system, the Kansas City park system, and Belle Isle Park in Detroit. When he died in 1903, the man with a passion for parks had done more than any American to soften the hard edges of city life for his contemporaries—and for generations to follow.

at night and on Sundays at Vaux's home in Manhattan.

The two shared a vision of the park as a scenic work of art that would combine a natural appearance with touches of the picturesque. Instead of a playground for the city's upper crust, they wanted a park where people of all social backgrounds would mingle and enjoy beautiful, uncontaminated surroundings. Olmsted, already on the job and beginning the cleanup of the site, had been over the terrain on horseback and was familiar with every swamp and rocky outcrop. He and Vaux would head for the park on moonlit nights to work out design problems on the spot. Vaux brought different strengths to the partnership. An accomplished architect tutored by Downing in the art of landscaping, he was also skilled at landscape drawing. This enabled him to make "before and after" sketches showing how dismal stretches of land could be transformed into delightful pastoral regions. The drawings were submitted along with the park design they titled "Greensward."

Their plan, the original of which can be seen on the third floor of the Arsenal, included an impressive variety of lawns, gardens, lakes, ponds, cascades and woodlands, all connected by curving paths, driveways, arches and bridges. One formal element, a long, straight mall ending in a magnificent lakeside terrace, was included. A unique aspect of the Greensward Plan was its treatment of traffic. Walks, drives

Architect and Prime Mover

Calvert Vaux

Calvert Vaux was described by a friend as "endowed with many of the inspirations and accomplishments of genius...an original artist."

Though often overshadowed by Frederick Olmsted, their collaboration on Central Park and other projects was one of coequals. It usually was Vaux who supplied the professional expertise and artistry, while Olmsted was the inspired park enthusiast and magnetic leader who brought their plans to fruition.

Vaux was well-educated and well-trained. Born in London in 1824, he was apprenticed at 19 to a leading architectural firm. In a few years, he gained a broad knowledge of architecture and sharpened his own professional skills. On a walking tour of France and Germany, he admired historic buildings and superb art but also visited villages and other country locales, whetting his interest in rural scenery.

and bridle paths were arranged so that they crossed each other over bridges or through tunnels, thus keeping pedestrian crossings to a minimum. To separate crosstown vehicular traffic from the park, the designers provided four sunken

Transverse roads such as this one through Vista Rock at 79th Street were designed to permit traffic to flow discreetly below the park via tunnels. They also serve to muffle street noise, adding to the overall tranquility of the park. Ingenious in design, these roads required teams of men working day and night, wielding pickaxes, shovels, dynamite and even cannonballs to blast through the dense rock outcroppings.

When Andrew Jackson Downing, the preeminent American landscape designer, visited London in 1850, he engaged the promising young architect as an assistant in his busy office in Newburgh, New York. Although the association ended with Downing's death only two years later, the experience proved rewarding for Vaux. As a protege of Downing, he had added landscape designing to his list of credentials.

Calvert Vaux

formal partnership was ended in 1872. Neither man ever lost respect or friendship for the other, but their ambitions differed. Although a recognized leader in the nascent American park movement, Vaux now chose to expand his architectural practice. He designed the original buildings of the Metropolitan Museum of Art and the American Museum of Natural History. He built residences, including the mansion for Samuel Tilden that still stands on New York's Gramercy Park as an outstanding example of Victorian architecture. Appalled at the slum conditions in New York, Vaux also designed model homes for the poor and shelters for the Children's Aid Society.

After moving to New York City in 1856, Vaux began his alliance with Olmsted. In their greatest achievement, the creation of Central Park, the two shared in the overall planning. Olmsted, as the park's tough-minded administrator, saw to it that things got done. The structures in the park, its bridges, arches, buildings, and the Terrace, were the work of Vaux, often assisted by Jacob Wrey Mould.

After Vaux and Olmsted went on to build Prospect Park in Brooklyn and a few other urban parks, their

At the same time, Vaux never lost interest in parks. In the 1880s, he rejoined the Department of Parks as landscape architect and at the time of his death, in 1895, he and Olmsted were designing a park for the city of Newburgh: Downing Park, named after Vaux's old mentor.

transverse roads whose noise and bustle would not be apparent to the parkgoers.

The competition drew thirty-three entrants, but on April 28, 1858, the Greensward Plan was judged the best. Olmsted, while continuing as Superintendent, now was named Architect-in-Chief of the park; Vaux was named Assistant to the Architect-in-Chief.

After winning the prize, the two partners confronted what must have seemed a monumental task. "Nature," said one observer, "had done nothing for this part of the island. It was bleak, dreary and sickly." Amid the many rocks were large patches of stagnant swampland. Squatters had denuded large areas of all vegetation except the tangled underbrush. To transform this site into a landscaped park would take a mighty effort.

Machinery was scarce, and so manpower and horsepower had to do the work. Pickaxes, hammers, shovels and gunpowder for blasting were the major tools. In the first five years, according to one estimate, park workers moved 2.5 million

cubic yards of stone and earth into or out of the park in horse-drawn cartloads. To create the transverse roads, they had to hack and blast their way through tough Manhattan schist and granite, cutting through some 300,000 cubic yards of the rock.

At the same time, other work gangs were building a drainage system that would support the park's plant life. All told, they installed some sixty-two miles of tile pipes three to four feet below the surface in many parts of the park. The tiles had perforated tops to catch water seeping through the turf and then feed it into the park's planned water bodies. Workers also drained the stagnant water in the swamps and turned up fertile subsoil for planting. In response to demands in the press for quick public benefits, they excavated one former bog area (now the Lake), built a terraced shore and piped in enough fresh water to have it ready for ice skating during the frigid winter of 1858-1859.

To revitalize the earth on the park site, an estimated half-million cubic yards of topsoil and 40,000 cubic

yards of fertilizing manure and compost were spread. Planting undoubtedly was watched over closely by Olmsted and Vaux, but the man most directly responsible for it was Ignaz Pilat. As chief gardener, this skilled Austrian horticulturalist supervised the planting of lawns, the selection and placement of trees and shrubs, the floral arrangements, even the shaping of slopes and positioning of boulders. Before work on the park began, only 42 species of trees were found in the area. By 1873, gardeners working under Pilat and his successors had planted an estimated four to five million trees, shrubs and vines. Among these plants were 402 species of deciduous trees and shrubs as well as a wide variety of evergreens such as pine, fir, spruce and cedar.

Work on the park went on throughout the 1860s, even during the Civil War, including the intervals when Olmsted and Vaux were not at the helm. In 1863, both resigned in a dispute with the Park Commission, particularly its strongest member, Andrew Haswell Green. First as the board's president, then as its comptroller, the formidable Green supported many of their visions for the park. But he was a determined pennypincher and autocrat who exercised—said Olmsted—a "systematic small tyranny" by questioning the cost of every proposed action. Despite this clash of wills, when Green asked the two to return to

In this 1863 photograph, a gatekeeper patrols an entrance to the still unfinished park. Sporting long gray coats with brass buttons, *the park keepers were disparagingly nicknamed "sparrow cops" because their park beat was deemed less dangerous than that of the city policemen.*

their park offices in 1865, they accepted his offer.

Though a difficult man, Green backed Olmsted and Vaux not only on most park policy but in their refusal to collude with venal Tammany Hall leaders. These politicians saw the park as a source of patronage jobs for their supporters and lucrative building contracts for their friends.

When Olmsted and Vaux returned to the park, the mammoth building project they launched a few years earlier was still functioning smoothly. Central Park was already attracting millions of visitors annually. Walking paths, carriage driveways, bridges, lawns, cascades and lakes had been created. The elm-lined Mall drew promenaders of all social classes and the Terrace, near completion, was much admired. Rowing on the Lake was enormously popular. At the weekends, large crowds gathered for concerts at a brightly painted bandstand.

The next few years proved fruitful for Olmsted and Vaux. The Loch and the Meer were finished, work on the perimeter wall neared completion and construction of the Gothic-style Belvedere Castle had begun. But the election of November 1868, which consolidated the power of William M. Tweed as Tammany leader, was bad news for the park. "Boss Tweed," as he was known, put thousands of unnecessary workers on the payroll and plans were made to place needless new buildings in pleasant verdant areas. In protest, both Olmsted and Vaux resigned in November of 1870.

The park suffered under Tweed's hand-picked officials. Thousands of trees were dug up and carted off to different parks for replanting, while

Once the park opened, a daily "carriage parade" became a popular pastime for the moneyed class.

others were damaged by incompetent pruning. Plantings carefully arranged to frame natural or architectural features were carelessly cleared away. Winding paths were straightened for "greater pedestrian convenience." Heedless of natural effect, workers scraped moss and lichen off the rocks in the Ramble.

Fortunately, the Tweed regime did not last long. Public outrage led to his downfall and imprisonment, and in November 1871, Olmsted and Vaux were called back to reassume command of the park. Back on the job, the two moved quickly to repair the damage. Expert gardening practices were restored and the building of the park moved ahead.

In 1873, Vaux resigned his park position to devote himself to other architectural and landscaping pursuits. In 1878, after a dispute with the board, Olmsted was dismissed after twenty years of association with the park. Fortunately, the building of Central Park was essentially completed and it was widely recognized that its design and building had been a monumental accomplishment.

Olmsted saw the park as a work of art, but he was not the only contributing artist. Calvert Vaux was his equal among the park's creators. Architect Jacob Wrey Mould (page 44) and chief gardener Ignaz Pilat (page 71), uniquely talented men who are all but forgotten today, did much to beautify it. And, of course, the existence of Central Park owed much to the engineers, artisans and laborers who supplied their skills and musclepower nearly a century and half ago.

SOUTH QUADRANT

Central Park South (59th St.) to 73rd Street

Map labels:

73 St.

72 St. — Womens' Gate — B,C — M10

Wisteria Arbors

Riftstone Arch

"Imagine" mosaic

71 St.

STRAWBERRY FIELDS

THE LAKE

Wisteria Arbor

Wagner Cove

Daniel Webster

70 St. — M10,72

Lawn Bowling and Croquet

Fa...

69 St.

7th Regiment Memorial

68 St. — M10,72

Mazzini

Playground

Mine... Spri...

Tavern on the Green

67 St. — CENTRAL PARK WEST

Fred Lebow

SCALE
One city bloc...
(north to sout...
equals approxim...
1/20th of a mile...
1/13th of a kilom...

SHEE...

66 St. — M10,72

65TH ST.

65 St.

TRANSVERS...

Ballfield (sea...

#6

Dalehead Arch

WEST DRIVE

#5 HECKSC... BALLFIE...

#4

#3

Umpire Rock

64 St.

63 St. — M10

62 St.

Pine Bank Arch

Hecks... Playg...

Mayflower Hotel

Greyshot Arch

61 St. — M10

Trump Int'l Hotel

A,B, C,D, 1, 9 — Merchants' Gate

Maine Monument

Columbus Circle — M5, 7 — M5, 7

Artisan... Ga...

Legend

TRANSVERSES — ROADWAYS

BRIDLE PATHS

POLICE CALL BOX | INFORMATION DESK | PUBLIC PHONE | FOOD SERVICE | POLICE STATION | RE... ROC...

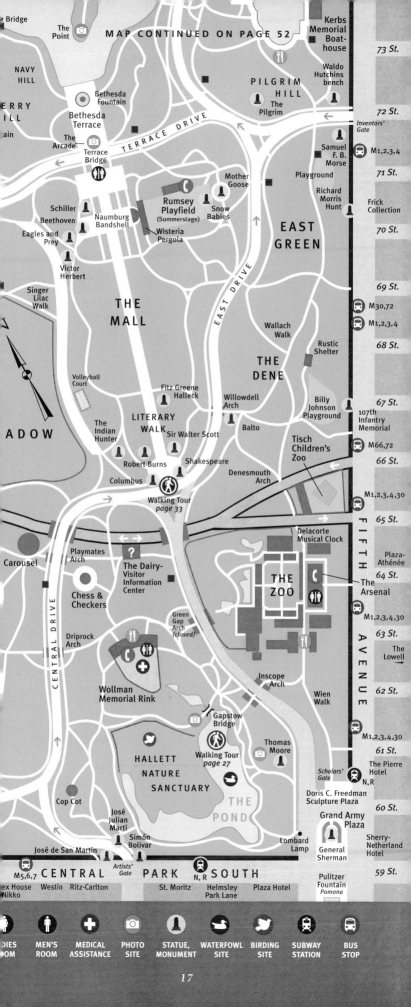

Grand Army Plaza

This magnificent space adjoining Fifth Avenue between 58th and 60th streets is well worth a brief exploration before entering the park at its southeast corner. Opposite the main entrance to the fabled Plaza Hotel stands the Pulitzer Memorial Fountain, a gift of the publisher of the old *New York World* and now a popular gathering spot. The multitiered marble fountain is crowned by Karl Bitter's graceful bronze figure of *Pomona*, the Roman goddess of abundance, who gazes down benevolently at an assortment of taxis, carriage horses, food vendors and sidewalk portrait artists.

General William Tecumseh Sherman Statue

Facing *Pomona* from the north is the sharply contrasting mounted figure of Union Army General William Tecumseh Sherman, one of the heroes of the American Civil War. Resplendent in gold leaf, the towering statue is the last major work of the distinguished American sculptor Augustus Saint-Gaudens. It won a Grand Prix at the Paris Exposition in 1900 and is considered one of the world's preeminent equestrian monuments.

The statue portrays Nike, the Greek goddess of victory, leading a confident, resolute Sherman on his march through Georgia, a bloody campaign that dealt a devastating blow to the South. The beautifully-muscled horse, its right rear hoof symbolically trampling a Georgia pine branch, moves briskly ahead along a rugged, inclined plane. The wind pressing the folds of Nike's gown against her legs also catches the mane and tail of the horse and Sherman's cape. Viewed from the side, the three indeed seem to be marching to victory.

Across the street and to the left of the park entry leading to The Pond, stands the Lombard Lamp. An ornate cast-iron lamppost, it is a replica of originals on the Lombard Bridge in the German city of Hamburg. It was presented by that city to the park in 1979 as a "bridge of friendship in human relations, trade and commerce."

In this famous statue by Saint-Gaudens, Union General William Tecumseh Sherman is led into battle against the Confederacy by Nike, Goddess of Victory. Brilliant in gold leaf, the American Civil War hero is resolute; his spirited mount symbolically treads on a branch of Georgia pine.

The Arsenal viewed from the south in 1862. Fifth Avenue is to the right. The Denesmouth Arch, in the background, stands north of the present-day Zoo.

Doris C. Freedman Plaza

Directly behind the Sherman statue is a lively area just outside the park entrance originally named the Scholars' Gate. It is now the setting for changing installations of contemporary American sculpture. The plaza was named in honor of an admired advocate of contemporary art who championed the "Percent For Art" program in New York City, whereby builders were encouraged to allocate funds for the commission or purchase of art for their sites.

The Arsenal

One of the park's historic buildings, the turreted Arsenal facing Fifth Avenue at 64th Street is headquarters of the city's Department of Parks and Recreation. Above its doorway is a fierce cast-iron eagle, guarding the building since it was erected by the State of New York in 1848 to store munitions. The ornamental drums flanking the door and the replica muskets on the stairway were added much later as part of a 1934 renovation.

The building is largely hived with working offices, including that of the Parks Commissioner, but the public is welcome and there are interesting things to see. In the lobby, the murals depicting scenes of old New York were painted during the Depression years 1935 and 1936 by artists funded by the Federal Works Progress Administration (WPA). But for most visitors, the central chamber on the third floor is the main attraction. Exhibits of paintings, sculpture or photography on subjects relating to New York or the park itself are presented regularly. Also notable are two large bronze eagles, originally part of the Prison Ship Martyrs Monument in Fort Greene Park, Brooklyn, but removed from that site due to persistent vandalism. On the wall in the conference room down the hall is the original Olmsted and Vaux "Greensward Plan" for the park. It can be viewed when the room is not in use.

The plan did not include the Arsenal, suggesting that the designers of Central Park expected to have it demolished. Many people at the time thought the building ugly. The noted diarist George Templeton Strong called it "hideous," an "eyesore," and hoped it would "soon be destroyed by accidental fire." Others proposed that the red-brick fortress be partially pulled down, with the remains arranged artfully to create picturesque ruins.

Despite the critics, city officials found the building useful, and in the early years of the park it was home to a police precinct, the embryonic American Museum of Natural History (now at Central Park West between 77th and 81st streets), a Gallery of Art and the Municipal Weather Bureau. At the same time, New Yorkers regarded the Arsenal as the perfect dumping ground for unwanted animals of all sorts. Dozens of cages crowded the basement and the grounds behind the building, where people flocked to marvel at a collection ranging from raccoons, foxes and porcupines to eagles, alligators and boa constrictors. Much admired were three African Cape Buffalo, a gift of General William Tecumseh Sherman, and a bear sent from the west by General George Custer.

This makeshift arrangement ended in 1871 when the animals were transferred to the newly constructed buildings of the park's first permanent menagerie. At the same time, the Arsenal was turned over to park offices and became an accepted, if largely ignored, part of the city landscape. Decades of neglect followed, and by the early 1920s the curious old building had become a shabby wreck, with broken windows, missing brickwork and a badly leaking roof. A headline in *The New York Times* read, "Parks Arsenal a Near Ruin."

Demolition was considered, but the building was given another lease on life with a minor renovation in 1924. A much greater boost came with the advent of Robert Moses as Parks Commissioner in 1934. Moses had a powerful personality and powerful friends, including such parklovers as former governor Alfred E. Smith, financier Bernard Baruch and Iphigene Ochs Sulzberger, whose father owned *The New York Times*. From his command center in the Arsenal, Moses not only carried out radical changes throughout the park but thoroughly overhauled and spruced up the Arsenal itself.

In the decades since Moses resigned in 1960, the building has taken on something of an emblematic quality. Movie-makers like to shoot films there. Protesters sporadically appear to publicize their causes. "Flower children" confronted one commissioner in his office and demanded—and were given—space on the Sheep Meadow for a vast "love-in." For the most part, however, the Arsenal is now the scene of earnest public forums and official business.

Among the residents of the Wildlife Center are colorful toucans (above), which greet visitors at the entrance of the Tropic Zone, and the entertaining Japanese snow monkeys (right) seen here on their island habitat in the Temperate Territory.

The once-scorned edifice, the oldest in the park except for the 1814-vintage stone Blockhouse, now enjoys the status of an official New York City Landmark, assuring it protection against the designs of any future partisans of the wrecking ball.

Wildlife Center and Zoo

A few short steps from Fifth Avenue, the Zoo—officially called the Central Park Wildlife Center—is one of the most popular attractions in New York City. And no wonder. People of all ages find it a magical place, with creatures ranging from rain forest denizens such as toucans, piranhas, tamarin monkeys and gila monsters to cooler-climate inhabitants like red pandas, sea lions, polar bears and a remarkable colony of penguins. Some of the simulated habitats created for the animals are stunningly realistic.

Since its radical redesign and reconstruction in the 1980s, the Zoo has won praise from the news media, the public and a usually hard-to-please community of wildlife experts.

The innovative layout of the Zoo is worthy of attention. Stretching around much of the central garden area where the sea lions cavort is an elegant brick colonnade topped by a wooden trellis and a connecting roof of opaque glass. The graceful structure forms a covered archway linking the major exhibit areas and buildings. All told, the Zoo's 5.5 acres are home to some 450 animals of over 100 different species; and whether they are indoors or out, not one is behind bars or in a cage.

The exhibits are grouped into three climatic zones—tropical, temperate and polar. Upon entering the Zoo, visitors often begin at the nearby Tropic Zone building.

Tropic Zone

Here you step into a remarkably naturalistic recreation of a tropical rain forest, complete with huge tree trunks, twisting vines, waterfalls, streams and a profusion of multi-colored plant life. Bird calls sound in the air. Look carefully. Up in the branches or darting from place to place you can see a great variety of birds—Turquoise Tanagers, Saffron Finches, Fairy Bluebirds, Sun Bitterns, Violet Turacos and many others. The dense greenery is also home to unusual tortoises and turtles, as well as the

big-winged Rodriguez Fruit Bats from an island in the Indian Ocean. You may see them hanging from the higher branches or fluttering about near the glass ceiling. Stairways provide a view of the forest scene from various levels.

Other, smaller exhibits in the building present a rich assortment of jungle life, including giant geckos, prehensile-tailed skinks, pythons and other lethal snakes, and frogs whose glands secrete poison for use on hunting darts. Flesh-hungry piranhas glare out of one watery habitat; muddy caimans, smaller relatives of the alligator, share a darkened space with a swarm of

bats. Of special, but far from exclusive, interest to children is a closeup display of thousands of leaf-cutter ants going about their job of slicing up leaves and hauling the pieces off to their underground realm. Intense activity in the ant tunnels is recorded by tiny cameras and shown on overhead TV screens.

Nearby, a troop of silky black and white Colobus monkeys rules over its own rocky domain. And upstairs on the second level, the extremely rare Black Lion Tamarin monkeys have their own bit of wilderness. These alert, leonine little primates were once thought to be extinct, but in 1970 they were "rediscovered" in

Playful North American River Otters (left) and a Chinese red panda (below) delight visitors in the Temperate Territory.

This aerial view (above left) shows the Zoo with its three climatic zones oriented around an elegant central garden and sea lion pool. A tour is not complete without a visit to the Polar Circle where polar bears hold court in an outdoor display area. Viewable from several levels, they can be seen pacing on "Arctic" rocks, playing with bear-size toys or swimming gracefully underwater. The nearby Penguin Building (left) features Gentoo and Chinstrap Penguins from the Antarctic in a climate-controlled environment, "The Edge of the Ice Pack." Feeding time is memorable as squeals of delight from young observers mingle with the high-pitched squawks of penguins.

the Brazilian rain forest. On display are three varieties: the rarest of all, the Black Lion Tamarin; and the slightly more numerous Golden-headed Tamarin and Cotton-top Tamarin.

Temperate Territory

After exiting the Tropic Zone building, the archway leads northward into the Temperate Territory. The first thing you see is a craggy island inhabited by Japanese macaques, or snow monkeys, the northernmost variety of this primate. They can be entertaining when in the mood. Except for these monkeys, the temperate area consists of a carefully landscaped garden containing a number of small ponds. On foot, or from benches along the pathways, visitors can watch Chinese red pandas, North American River Otters and a variety of water birds, fish and turtles.

Polar Circle Denizens

The northern edge of the temperate territory connects with the last major climatic area, the Polar Circle. First come the polar bears, attention-riveting as they pace, sprawl or swim in their spacious open-air quarters. Visitors can view these admirable but highly dangerous beasts through a glass partition below the pool surface, from ground

level and from a platform above. A separate, adjacent polar setting is home to spotted harbor seals and Arctic foxes.

Moving on, you next reach the Penguin Building and a delightful display called "The Edge of the Ice Pack." An ingenious design, it includes areas of land and ice as well as a saltwater sea that periodically ripples with small waves. Viewers do not feel it, but the air in the climate-controlled display is kept comfortably frosty for the small group of plump, comic-looking North Atlantic tufted puffins and—the star attraction—a large congregation of Gentoo and Chinstrap Penguins. These appealing creatures from the Antarctic waddle around like friendly villagers or take to the water and zoom about at amazing speed, an underwater performance you can watch through the glass partition. It's a hard act to follow, but the sea lions in the central garden area are equal to the challenge.

Sea Lions at Center Court

On the rock ledges or in the large pool, these hefty marine mammals from California are a treat to watch. Their acrobatics in the water are especially impressive, and occasionally good for a surprise. One after-

noon, a sea lion actually splashed to the surface with a revolver in its mouth. Generally, a good time to see them is at feeding time: 11:30 a.m., 2:00 p.m., and 4 p.m.

The Wildlife Conservation Society (formerly called The New York Zoological Society), which operates the Zoo, likes to stress that it is not solely for amusement but for learning about wildlife. The Intelligence Garden, a pleasant leafy area off the archway a few steps east of the Tropic Zone Building, has therefore been set aside so that school groups or casual visitors can hear informative talks by wildlife experts. (The name of the garden was borrowed from the Chinese Emperor Wen Chang, who in 1100 B.C. showed wild animals on a section of his palace grounds to enlighten his subjects about nature.) In addition, the Zoo School, located just to the north of the Arsenal, has a series of appealing programs designed chiefly for children from preschoolers to teenagers.

As might be imagined, today's Central Park Zoo—with its state-of-the-art habitats, humane conditions for the animals and concern for enlightenment as well as amusement—is a great improvement over past conditions.

By 1873, the Menagerie attracted more than two-and-one-half million people. Murphy the hippo and Mike the chimp were particular favorites.

the location of the present Zoo.

From the start, the Menagerie, as it was called, was hugely popular. In 1873, it had more than two-and-one-half million visitors, roughly a quarter of all parkgoers. Though critics complained of the "rabble" the Menagerie attracted, New Yorkers of every social status loved to gawk at the kangaroos, monkeys, and other exotic creatures. Particularly admired were "Murphy" the hippo and "Mike Crowley," the first chimpanzee ever shown in the United States. Whenever the celebrity chimp took sick, letters of sympathy, along with favorite home cures, poured in; people would come to pray outside his cage for "Mr." Crowley's recovery.

Despite the popularity of the Menagerie, a series of inattentive city governments in the decades of the late 19th and early 20th centuries left it in a sorry condition. The buildings became dilapidated, rust corroded the bars of the cages, and the health of the animals was neglected. According to nature writer Eugene Kinkead, "The exhibits included a puma with rickets, a palsied baboon, and a tiger with senile dementia."

On taking office as Parks Commissioner in Fiorello La Guardia's reform government in 1934, master-builder Robert Moses moved with his usual dispatch. In less than a year, the "hideous old sheds," as *The*

Forerunner of the Zoo

In the early years of the park, a zoo of sorts sprang into being almost by accident when people began to leave unwanted animals at the Arsenal, where they were kept in cages in the basement or in the area behind the building. In 1870, permanent quarters in the form of five wooden buildings filled with cages were established for the animals in the area west of the Arsenal, roughly

The first elephant in the makeshift zoo in 1866

With its bronze animals parading merrily around the clock tower every hour and half hour, the Delacorte musical clock beckons to visitors of all ages, making it one of the most popular sights in the park.

New York Times described the Menagerie, were demolished and replaced by a "brand-new brick-and-concrete zoo." The shiny new buildings, an attractive open square surrounding a sea lion pool, and the healthy, well-cared-for animals were welcomed by the press and public. The cafeteria, especially the terrace with its umbrellas and striped awnings, became a favored meeting place for European exiles during the 1930s and 1940s.

In the years following World War II, a succession of municipal governments once again allowed the Zoo to deteriorate. Moreover, ideas about zoos and the display of animals had changed, leading wildlife experts and advocates of humane animal treatment to condemn the once-applauded Moses zoo. The critics particularly complained that the animals were confined in cages with concrete floors and limited outdoor space. With little room to run, jump or romp with their cohorts, the animals grew listless and weak. Some

had only boards to sleep on.

In the face of mounting criticism, in 1982 the Parks Department announced that the Zoo would be totally redesigned to bring it "into the 20th century with animals maintained in an ambiance that is suitable and responsible." A complete renovation took several years, and the unique and widely acclaimed Zoo you see today was opened in August 1988.

The Delacorte Clock

Atop the brick arcade over the pathway between the main zoo area and the Children's Zoo is one of the delights of the park: the Delacorte musical clock. Every hour and half hour, two bronze monkeys bang their hammers against the great bell on top. Then, to a merry children's tune such as "Three Blind Mice" or "The Parade of the Wooden Soldiers," six other bronze animals—a penguin and his drum, a fiddling hippo, a bear and his tambourine, a concertina-playing elephant, a goat with pipes and a horn-tooting kangaroo—dance and play their way around the clock tower.

The donor of this appealing musical clock tower was publisher, philanthropist and park benefactor George T. Delacorte. Captivated by musical clocks he had seen in Europe, he commissioned this work; the animal figures were created by Italian sculptor Andrea Spadini.

Tisch Children's Zoo

Just a few paces north of the Delacorte Clock is the Children's Zoo, re-opened in 1997 after a complete makeover sponsored by philanthropist Laurence A. Tisch. For a sample taste of the wonderland ambiance inside, have a look at the decorative bronze work over the outer entrance gate. Sculpted by Paul Manship, this captivating memento of the original Lehman Children's Zoo is composed of stylized branches, fanciful birds, and small boys playing Pan pipes and capering with dancing goats.

To enter the zoo, children (and adults) must find their way through the trunk of a huge make-believe tree. Visitors then find themselves on a pathway winding among flowering shrubs, lilting streams, watersprays and waterfalls. On right and left are giant mock turtles, acorns and dragonflies, as well as real birds perching, paddling or flying about freely. To restrain those Crested Doves, Hooded Mergansers, Golden Pheasants and Sacred Ibises which might wish to leave this miniature Eden, an enclosing tent of near-invisible wire mesh stretches overhead.

For the very young, marvels are everywhere. In little ponds, Painted Turtles, Red-Eared Turtles and Bullfrogs swim and sun themselves. Nearby, a small community of Dutch, Rex and Lop-Eared Rabbits mingle peaceably outside their hutches. And steps away, imitation turtle shells and hollowed-out stone rabbits await—for young visitors to crawl into, look out of, and have a picture taken in.

Go through another tree trunk passage and you find yourself in an unscreened space, where children can climb around on a spiderweb of black rope or feed barnyard animals. Machines dispense dry, crunchy animal food for 25 cents. Separate pens hold Vietnamese Pot-Bellied Pigs, a black Dexter Cow, and a variety of lambs and goats. All of them, and particularly the perky, gray African Pygmy Goats, seem happy to accept the food as well as the pats from numerous small hands.

Before leaving the children's zoo, you may encounter one of its big, multi-colored, talking birds. These amiable creatures (zoo volunteers in costume) like to talk to children (and even adults). They answer questions, pose for pictures and often make you, or a child with you, promise to come back again.

Since its opening, attendance at the zoo has far exceeded expectations, so arrive early, remember that weekdays are less congested than weekends and leave your stroller at the parking facility outside the front gate. A small admission fee to the children's zoo can be paid separately or included as part of your visit to both zoos. Open seven days, Monday through Friday: 10:00 a.m. to 5:00 p.m. Weekends: 10:30 a.m. to 5:30 p.m.

⑤ A Tour of the Pond

One of the prettiest ornaments of the park, the serpentine body of water in its southeast corner is simply called The Pond. Miraculously shielded from nearby city noise by inspired landscaping that includes a sheltering abundance of tall trees and shrubs, it is an inviting place to stroll or claim a bench along the pathway.

Gapstow Bridge

Curving over the Pond's northern neck is Gapstow Bridge, a sturdy structure well placed for an overview of the pond and its surroundings. It also is an excellent place to snap pictures. To the south, the tall skyscrapers of midtown Manhattan stand in stark contrast to the verdant beauty of the park and frame the elegant tops of landmarks like the Plaza and Essex House hotels. On the Pond's eastern side, in a picturesque landscape of dark rock, tall trees and well-tended grassy slopes, a network of pathways parallels the water's edge. To the west, the view is dominated by a rugged, forested bluff called the Promontory in earlier years; it is now the Hallett Nature Sanctuary.

Observing this terrain today, it is not easy to picture the unhealthy swampland it was in pre-park days. The area was called Pigtown, where a dozen or so immigrant households lived in squalor. Through the boggy land flowed De Voor's Mill Stream, a shallow rivulet that emptied eventually into the East River.

Creating the park changed all that. Squatters were evicted. Swamps were drained. The water flow from the stream was used to make the "lake of irregular shape" we now know as

The Pond. Incidentally, the stream still flows underground, beneath the Pond and the subbasements of skyscrapers on Fifth Avenue.

For a closer look at the Pond and its setting, a leisurely walk around its rim is suggested. Leaving the bridge, head south along the eastern bank. You will pass numerous Pin Oak and Black Locust trees and dense thickets of shrubs, chief among them a variety of Cotoneaster, an evergreen member of the rose family. These shrubs attract birds of many kinds, including the common sparrow and starlings which often inhabit them in great number.

After a short distance, a stairway off to the left leads to the Inscope Arch, one of Calvert Vaux's elegant creations. Made of pink and gray granite, the thirty-four-foot-long Tuscan archway is nestled secretly in the landscape and not heavily used. Clean and well-lit, it is a safe, quick route to the Zoo and the Arsenal.

Statue of Thomas Moore
Further along the waterside is another path, on which a short eastward detour takes you to a bronze bust of the Irish poet Thomas Moore sculpted by Dennis Sheahan. Considered the national bard of Ireland in the early 19th century, Moore was a close friend and biographer of Lord Byron. In addition to verse, Moore wrote such songs as "The Last Rose of Summer" and "The Minstrel Boy."

Returning again to the water's edge, many visitors use this scenic vista to admire the skyline and take pictures. It is also a good spot to consider the Pond itself. Once five acres in extent, it was reduced to 3.5 acres in 1951, when the northern tip was filled in to make room for the Wollman Rink (page 30). Until 1924, swan boats, like those still found in the Boston Public Garden, took passengers on unhurried tours of the Pond.

Real swans were also fairly com-

A favored spot of photographers, painters and sightseers, the slope just north of Gapstow Bridge affords an unparalleled view that contrasts the serenity of the park landscape with the monumentality of the city looming beyond.

especially when local residents or visitors offer a bit of soft pretzel or leftover bread from a park lunch. It was on this very spot that Macaulay Culkin first encountered the "Pigeon Lady" in the 1992 movie, *Home Alone 2—Lost in New York.*

Resuming the walk, after passing a large rock fringed with forsythia and bayberry on the right, the pathway turns west along the peaceful southern edge of the Pond. Even in the mid-19th century, the horse-and-buggy traffic on 59th Street was noisy, and Olmsted was determined to shield this site from the city's clamor. Fortunately, the waterline was considerably below the level of the street. So he ordered the building of a substantial earthen slope from the edge of the path to the foot of the wall along Central Park South. On it, a good many shrubs and tall white ash trees were planted, a landscaping strategy that still works today, muting the sounds of the street and keeping the bustle of the city at bay.

Soon after bearing westward around the big rock, strollers will find a delightful, sweeping view of the Pond at the pipe-rail on the water's edge. Ivy-covered Gapstow can be seen across the water in the distance. Directly opposite the pipe-rail is the densely-wooded sanctuary, its shoreline heavily grown with phragmite reeds. (These "exotic" European reeds are much deplored by some ecologists as "the scourge of the wetland," because they crowd out native plant life and presumably disturb the natural ecosystems.) On a more prosaic note, right below the railing the overflow from the Pond can be seen draining into the underground conduits that take it several miles to the Newtown Creek Treatment Plant in Brooklyn. After purification it is then released into the East River.

As the path continues westward, you will pass yew hedges, inkberry and viburnum shrubs, and a medley of trees—sour gums, cedars, willow oaks, crab apples, honey locusts, and Chinese scholar trees. The last are notable for their dark, furrowed bark and cream-colored summer

mon sights. Back in the 1860s, the first of them arrived, gifts of the German city of Hamburg and the Royal Companies of Vintners and Dyers of London. Over the years, the lordly white birds frequented the Pond, where they seemed to delight in gliding near the shore and staring down dogs being walked on the pathway. Today, because of maltreatment, swans have become a rarity throughout the park, reduced to a single pair that patrol the Lake. The waters of the Pond have been left to the plentiful ducks and geese that stop off on their annual migrations. Mallards, Black Ducks, Ruddy Ducks, Buffleheads, Canada Geese, and the infrequent Wood Duck can be seen and fed at most times of the year. In the springtime, proud mother Mallards are often seen instructing their newborns in the ways of the wild. Egrets and herons can occasionally be sighted fishing on the western shoreline.

Pigeons often crowd the walk,

flowers. After the pathway bends to the north, only a dwindling arm of the Pond now separates it from the bank of the Hallett sanctuary. Before proceeding around its fenced perimeter, however, you may wish to take the path leading up the hill on the left to a rustic summerhouse called the Cop Cot. A 1985 replica of one built in the early 1860s, its curious name is old Anglo-Saxon for "hilltop cottage." In good weather, it is a popular spot for an outdoor brown-bag lunch. Notice the spiked-leaved plantings on its southern side. Yucca, or Spanish Bayonet as it is also called, grows well in this location's rocky soil and offers the visitor a chance to view the rare desert plant in the wild.

Hallett Nature Sanctuary

Returning to the perimeter of the nature sanctuary, the path follows it northward, then turns east. Along this stretch, it is possible to peer through the chain-link fence for a glimpse of the rocky, four-acre woodland. Once called the Promontory because its high, bulky mass jutted into the Pond, it was a popular hiking and climbing site until it was closed to the public and set aside as the Bird Sanctuary in 1934. It was renamed the Hallett Nature Sanctuary in 1986, in honor of George Hervey Hallett, Jr., a prominent New York civic leader and "an ardent nature lover."

Inside the fence, the many shrubs, Black Cherry trees, wildflowers and other vegetation have been allowed to grow untended, providing a mini-wilderness for animals and plant life. Woodchucks, in particular, have flourished. Rabbits and raccoons are sometimes seen. Migratory birds prefer the Ramble and the North Woods to the sanctuary these days, presumably because it is too close to noisy 59th Street and has become—it is said—a hunting ground for feral cats. But the Park Rangers, who conduct guided tours of the sanctuary and many other parts of the park, report that some of the migratories still drop in and that year-round species such as sparrows, blue jays, downy woodpeckers and chickadees are very much in evidence. By some accounts, regular visitations are also made after dark by sharp-beaked night herons, who swoop down into the sanctuary to fish by moonlight along the edge of the Pond.

As you come to the end of the wire fence, the tour around the Pond returns you to our starting point: Gapstow Bridge.

Wollman Rink

The park's first skating rink—named after philanthropist Kate Wollman—has had its ups and downs since it opened in 1951. But from the start New Yorkers and visitors loved it, as they do today.

During every ice-skating season (mid-October through early April), hundreds of thousands of people of all ages glide or totter around the ice to a stream of exhilarating music. The admission price is modest. Skaters either bring or rent skates, and instruction classes are available. In addition to exercise under the open skies against a stunning backdrop of greenery and skyscrapers, the rink provides an exceptional site for an outing with friends and a chance to make new ones.

This happy state of affairs also prevailed before 1980, but then the refrigerating system broke down and renovation became necessary. The city government promised it would be ready in two years, and a builder did promptly install a new "state-of-the-art" system. But the twenty-nine miles of pipes, filled with the refrigerant freon and covered by newly-laid concrete, soon sprang hundreds of mysterious leaks. Long investigations and high-priced studies were made, years passed, and no one could pinpoint the cause of the problem.

By the summer of 1986, as skaters fumed and Parks Department officials guessed that it might take years more to solve the problem, Donald Trump asked for and was given the job. When the real estate titan promised to finish it by mid-December, he met with enormous skepticism. But Trump knew how to get things built. Contractors appeared as if by magic. Work proceeded rapidly. He replaced the freon with the previously-used brine solution, mended the pipes, poured fresh concrete, and had the rink open and in sparkling condition a month earlier than his target date.

The 33,000-square-foot rink, reputedly the largest artificial ice-skating surface in North America, has been open for business and public pleasure ever since. In recent years, the rink has been used for inline roller skating from mid-April to early July. Admission prices and

The Dairy, constructed in 1870 to provide city children with milk from sanitary farms, is now the main information center for visitors.

daily schedules may vary over the year. For information, the rink management suggests calling (212) 396-1010.

The Dairy

Designed by Vaux and erected in 1870, the Dairy has been since its inception one of the major centers of activity in the lower Park. In its early years, the picturesque building situated just south of the 65th Street transverse road was the hub of what Olmsted called the Children's District. Since a much-needed renovation was completed in 1980, the Dairy has served as the park's Visitor Center. A stop here is highly recommended, either for information and exhibits about the park, or for its architectural and historic interest.

In creating the Children's District, the park's designers furnished it with an appealing mixture of buildings. As you will note, the Dairy itself is an amalgam of styles favored in the 19th century. The stone cottage, with its gambrel roof and vaguely church-style windows, has been called Victorian Gothic. The connected loggia, an airy, open gallery with a steeply-pitched roof and cutout railings, would be at home on an alpine chalet.

Other buildings Olmsted and Vaux placed nearby included a large rustic shelter on a hill they named the Kinderberg or Children's Mountain, and a gaily-decorated, musical Carousel that delighted New York's children.

The Dairy, though, was meant not only for amusement. At the time of Central Park's creation, thousands of New York children were dying each year from the tainted milk of cows kept in unsanitary conditions in the city. An important function of the Dairy was to have fresh milk brought in from approved farms outside the city and made available at minimal cost. For years, this mission was accomplished, as many thousands of mothers took their children to drink milk at tables on the loggia. In time, public demand led the Dairy to expand its offerings to include more adult fare, including coffee, sandwiches, ale and porter.

Far more damaging changes were to befall the Dairy in the early decades of the 20th century. With wholesome milk no longer difficult to find, its original social purpose had vanished. Besides, the general neglect of the park by successive city governments applied to the Dairy as well. It was closed to the public, vandalized and gradually allowed to decay. By the 1950s, the loggia had been totally demolished and the forlorn stone cottage was being used as an equipment storehouse. A metal cow mounted on a weathervane was the only clue to the Dairy's former identity.

The decline of the park, and of the Dairy in particular, was finally halted during the late 1970s by enlightened city governments in collaboration with the newly established Central Park Conservancy. Fueled in part by financing from private foundations, the Parks Department rallied preservationists, historians and architects behind the reclamation of the Dairy. Practitioners of such moribund crafts as stone masonry, slate roofing and ornamental carpentry were put to work. The restoration of the cottage was finished in 1979 and the loggia in 1981, both with striking success. For information, call (212) 794-6564.

Chess and Checkers

A short distance to the southwest of the Dairy, perched on the large rock outcropping once known as the Kinderberg, is the Chess and Checkers House. Built with a gift from financier Bernard Baruch in 1952, the octagonal red and cream colored brick structure has indoor and outdoor tables that attract players of all ages and skill. Playing pieces can be borrowed at the Dairy. In the summer, six- to thirteen-year-olds are taught to play chess by experts provided by the Conservancy. For information call (212) 794-6564.

The Kinderberg

Originally part of the park's Children's District, the Kinderberg was once the site of the largest rustic summer house in the park. Another of Vaux's creations, it measured 110 feet in diameter, and under its framework of cedar logs, twisted branches and vines were corridors and compartments with rough-hewn benches and tables for games. The inside perimeter of the shelter was

kept clear of furniture to give children "a running stretch of several hundred feet." An enchanting place, it was a temporary escape from city streets or crowded tenements.

The Carousel

As you walk west from the Chess and Checkers House and through the Playmates Arch under the park's Center Drive, you may begin to hear the distinctive calliope music of the Carousel. One of the country's largest merry-go-rounds, its fifty-eight hand-carved, brightly caparisoned horses and two ornate chariots are a sight to behold. Wonderful examples of folk art, they were made by Solomon Stein and Harry Goldstein in 1908. The Carousel is open seven days a week, weather permitting, and for ninety cents you can climb aboard for an exhilarating three-and-a-half minute whirl.

A merry-go-round has been delighting people on the same spot since the early days of the park. In the 1870s, it was turned by a blind mule and a horse in the basement, who would trot or stop as signalled by stomps on the floor above. Over the years, much more advanced and humane methods were introduced. In 1951, the Carousel was overhauled and given state-of-the-art equipment with a gift from the Michael Friedsam Foundation. Further renovation was made in 1982 with a donation from Alan and Katherine Stroock "in return for many happy go-rounds."

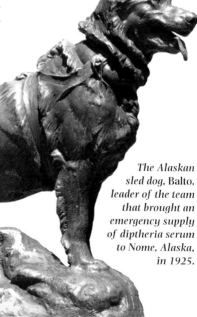

The Alaskan sled dog, Balto, leader of the team that brought an emergency supply of diptheria serum to Nome, Alaska, in 1925.

Since the 19th century, parents have found a few exhilarating whirls on the Carousel an ideal way to spend an afternoon with their children.

Statue of Balto

One of the most admired statues in the park is a memorial to a heroic dog: Balto. In 1925, when the isolated city of Nome, Alaska, was stricken by an epidemic of diptheria, the black malamute led a sled team of huskies through a blinding Arctic blizzard on the long final leg of a 655-mile run to deliver supplies of an antitoxin. The medicine saved thousands of lives. "I couldn't see the trail," said team driver Gunnar Kasson. "I gave Balto, my lead dog, his head and trusted him...It was Balto who led the way. The credit is his."

The larger-than-life bronze statue of Balto stands on a pedestal of bedrock outside the eastern portal of the Willowdell Arch, between Fifth Avenue and the Mall at the level of 67th Street. It shows him in harness, panting from exertion, yet poised for another dash. Decades of climbing and stroking have given a bright, golden hue to the ears, back and tail of the indomitable husky. A bas-relief plaque on the stone below shows the seven sled dogs on the historic run to the relief of Nome. The sculptor, Frederick G. R. Roth, was awarded the 1925 Speyer Prize by the National Academy of Design for this work.

A Tour of the Mall

A straight, tree-lined promenade slanting from just north of the 65th Street transverse to the Bethesda Terrace, the Mall is something of an oddity. It is formal and elegant, unlike much of the naturalistic landscape in the park. It has even been described as an "open air cathedral of elms." Yet Olmsted and Vaux also meant the Mall to be a hospitable meeting place, an "open air hall of reception" where large numbers of people of all ranks and preferences could mingle freely and peaceably.

The dual esthetic and social nature of the Mall is very much in evidence today. Under the archway of towering branches, or along the neighboring pathways, strollers admiring the flora or statuary coexist with exuberant teenagers and nannies shepherding their toddlers. Concertgoers heading for the Naumburg Bandshell have learned to dodge skateboarders and inline skaters of formidable, sometimes alarming, dexterity. But if the Mall has something of a split personality, it remains one of the park's most frequented locales, a magnet for New Yorkers and visitors alike.

One good way to approach the Mall is from its southern end. There an artfully arranged circular garden of shrubs and flowers is flanked on the east by a fine statue of a pensive Shakespeare by John Quincy Adams Ward and on the west by a bronze of a pious, elderly Columbus by Jeronimo Suñol. A short detour down the path to the west takes you to another work by Ward, *The Indian Hunter*, one of the more popular sculptures in the park since its unveiling in 1869.

Literary Walk
After returning to the Mall, more statues await along the "Literary Walk." Facing each other are bronzes of Robert Burns and Sir Walter Scott, both by Sir John Steell and gifts of Scottish residents of New York City in the 1870s. Burns, the ploughman-poet best known for songs such as "Auld Lang Syne," "Tam O'Shanter," and "My Heart's In the Highlands," is shown seated on a tree stump. He is thinking of his beloved Mary Campbell, dead at an early age, to whom he has written the poem inscribed on the scroll at his feet. Scott, enormously popular in the 19th century for romantic historical novels such as *Ivanhoe*, *Rob Roy* and *Quentin Durward*, sits at his ease with wrinkled stockings and carelessly tied shoes, a favorite hound at his side.

A short distance further along the

Mall is a statue of Fitz Greene Halleck, a minor 19th century American poet whose work is scarcely remembered today. The bronze, sculpted by James Wilson Alexander MacDonald, is notable chiefly for having a suitably minor American President, Rutherford B. Hayes, present at its unveiling in 1877. Hordes of spectators did so much damage to the Mall area that Olmsted denounced them as "essentially a mob, lawless and uncontrollable" and park officials prohibited any further ceremonies of the sort.

As you proceed northward, the spacious Mall, flanked by majestic elms, sweeps ahead, providing one of the finest scenes in the park. How different from the sight in pre-park days, when the area was largely a smelly swamp. The boggy land had to be filled in with chunks of hard schist bedrock blasted from nearby areas and covered with four feet of topsoil before the double rows of American elms were planted. Beneath their branches, battalions of laborers and craftsmen then built the quarter-mile-long Mall that points like an arrow to the Terrace and beyond to the forested Ramble.

On either side of the Mall, they also laid out areas of

The statue of the 19th century poet Fitz Greene Halleck

Rows of elm trees raise a leafy canopy high over the Mall. A formal and elegant promenade lined with benches and statues of literary figures, it offers a quiet spot to read, eat lunch or to simply watch the passing parade of visitors.

grassy turf, where over the years many more trees have been added, most of them elms. These elms, together with those that line the eastern boundary of the park along Fifth Avenue, constitute one of the largest stands of American elms left in the country. They deserve a nod of encouragement from passersby. In recent decades, Dutch elm disease has killed over half the American elms on the continent. It is a struggle, but the park's arboriculturists—with constant inspections, fungicide injections, pruning of infected limbs, and removal of terminally sick trees— have managed to keep losses down to roughly one percent a year. When a tree is removed, a young elm is planted in its place.

The Concert Ground

Moving along toward the upper end of the Mall, we come to an area that has been and continues to be a center of socializing and special events in the park. This is where the formal avenue broadens out both to the east and west, creating what was called—and still is by some—the Concert Ground. Today it is a decidedly hybrid scene, encompassing the Naumburg Bandshell, a cluster of green islands with curiously

designed benches, an asphalt expanse much prized by skaters, some statues of cultural icons, the Wisteria Pergola and the ornate entrance to the stairway leading to Bethesda Terrace.

From the start, this was a place for music. Slightly to the west of the Mall's main axis was a gracefully decorative cast-iron bandstand designed by Jacob Wrey Mould (page 44). In the summer, free weekly concerts of classical selections and contemporary melodies played by Harvey B. Dodworth's band drew large crowds. Some sat on the grass, others on benches or in their carriages. For the comfort and delight of the concertgoers, in the early 1870s Vaux installed ornamental drinking fountains, planting urns and bird cages. For ten cents, their children could take rides along nearby pathways in little carriages drawn by teams of goats.

By all accounts, the crowds who came to the concerts were mostly middle-class, though newspapers described some of them as "richly dressed ladies" and "elegantly attired gentlemen." Since the concerts at first were held only on Saturday, few unskilled workers, who usually had to put in a full six-day week, were in attendance. Not until 1884 did the

Above: A panoramic view of the Mall, looking south, in 1902

Left: Free Saturday after-noon concerts, performed in an ornate bandstand seen here under construc-tion, often drew upwards of 45,000 people to the Mall. At the insistence of working class New Yorkers, the park expanded the concert schedule to include Sunday—their only day off!

park commissioners submit to growing public demand and permit regular Sunday afternoon concerts. After that, reported the German-American newspaper *Staats-Zeitung*, working people made up the majori-ty of the Sunday concert crowds, while the Saturday events attracted "better society...in their velvet and silk." To the dismay of some old-line New Yorkers, large numbers of German-speaking immigrants, many of them skilled artisans, flocked to the concerts. As the years passed, other immigrant groups, chiefly Italians and Yiddish-speaking Jews, joined the audience, filling the air with what one newspaper called "a babel of tongues." The American novelist William Dean Howells not-ed that the Mall was packed with "mostly foreigners." But he approved of the "cosmopolitan" tone created by the immigrants. "For me," he wrote, "they all unite to form a spec-tacle I never cease to marvel at."

Another observer in the 1890s expressed his annoyance with the number of "monuments of foreign-ers" in the area. Quite possibly the chief source of his displeasure was Henry Bearer's large, glowering bust of Ludwig van Beethoven, the great German composer, which was installed west of the bandstand in 1884. Proud of their cultural her-itage, German-Americans had also presented the park with a portrait bust of poet and philosopher Johann von Schiller by the sculptor C.L. Richter. The first piece of sculpture in the park, it was placed in the Ramble in 1859 and moved in 1953 to its present spot next to Beethoven.

In fact, the Mall and its vicinity have been sites for statues since the park opened. In 1863, Christian Fratin's *Eagles and Prey*, a forceful depiction of two giant birds killing a trapped goat, was placed where it stands to this day. A short distance north of that is a bust of Victor

Herbert, composer of popular light operas such as *Babes in Toyland* and *The Red Mill*. Sculpted by Edmond T. Quinn and unveiled in 1927, the bronze shows Herbert facing the Concert Ground, where he had often conducted as bandmaster in the earlier years of the century.

Naumburg Bandshell

A major change was made in 1922, when the delicate Mould bandstand was demolished and replaced the following year by a far more substantial neoclassical limestone bandshell. A gift of banker Elkan Naumburg, the new bandshell was—and is—located on the eastern edge of the Mall, directly beneath the Wisteria Pergola. To accommodate larger audiences, a number of elms were cut down, some benches were removed, and a considerable space was paved with asphalt.

Not everyone was happy with the changes. When not in use, the area reminded some of an empty parking lot. But it served admirably as an outdoor dance hall when popular music was played. When the Edwin Franko Goldman Band appeared, as it did during the summertime from 1923 to 1969, the Parks Department would drag out benches and arrange them fan-like before the stage. Thousands would come from all over the city to catch a few breezes, eat a popsicle or two and delight in the marches, arias and show tunes. And all for free.

Besides the Goldman Band, opera companies and jazz, Latin and rock bands performed at the Naumburg Bandshell over the years. But as a result of increasingly noisy and rowdy behavior at pop concerts, in the mid-1980s park rules were changed to "discourage or rule out" hard rock and disco concerts, commercial or political events, and all programs likely to attract more than 2500 people. To control the decibel level, a major complaint of residents near the park, concert organizers were required to use the Parks Department's own sound system and sound technicians. Challenged in the courts, the noise regulations were upheld by the U.S. Supreme Court in 1989.

Despite the tighter rein, music continued to flourish in the park. In the late 1980s, a new festival called Summerstage was introduced at the Naumburg. Featuring an eclectic mix of music and other cultural events in the summer months, it quickly attracted overflow audiences. After a few seasons, Summerstage was moved to the more spacious Rumsey Playfield (page 38), where its programs of opera, dance and concerts by bands from around the world are performed each year from June through August in an outdoor theater with wooden bleachers. Other free musical events and dances are held at the plaza of the Charles A. Dana Discovery Center on the Harlem Meer. Both the Metropolitan Opera and the New York Philharmonic give free performances every summer on the Great Lawn.

In the early 1990s, the Parks Department and the Conservancy embarked on an ambitious program to restore the grounds near the bandshell to a more park-like condition. A sizable chunk of the asphalt area was replaced with islands of grassy turf, additional elm trees and a number of large decorative urns. For historic flavor, the perimeter of each island was lined by wooden benches based on drawings by Calvert Vaux. Among the park benches of the world, they are unique.

Dealing with the bandshell was a more painful task. In recent years, the once revered "Temple of Music" had fallen into near ruin, a graffiti-scarred nightime haunt of vandals and drug dealers. To some, it was an outdated eyesore, not worth the cost of renovating and policing. But when park leaders proposed to tear it down, a Coalition to Save the Naumburg Bandshell took the issue to court and won. According to the law, said the courts, philanthropic gifts to the city could not be destroyed.

The bandshell was saved, and the Parks Department has tried to make the best of it. At present, it permits events to be staged there, including band concerts, theater and dance, but applicants must be reviewed by several levels of park officials before an okay is given. If they do not agree to abide by rules concerning noise, conduct and size of audience, they are rejected out of hand. Scheduling is uncertain, so casual visitors to the Mall may or may not find something happening on the stage. But they are almost certain to find inline skaters whizzing about nearby, so it's best to be on guard.

Wisteria Pergola

Before leaving the Mall area, a quick inspection of the Wisteria Pergola— a small but notable piece of land-scape architecture—is suggested. Facing eastward, with the stairway to the Terrace on your left, take the flight of stairs next to the northern end of the bandshell up to the rustic arbor covered by Chinese wisteria. The thick vines that clasp the wooden framework date from the beginning of the park. One of the earliest specimens of this plant in the United States, its hanging clusters of lilac-colored flowers are a beautiful sight in early springtime. A slow walk through the arbor on a fine day is one of the park's nicer experiences.

Rumsey Playfield

A spartan, grassless rectangle between the northern end of the

Mall and the East Drive, the Mary Harriman Rumsey Playfield is used for school sports during much of the year. It is also the home of Summerstage, which presents a series of free musical events each year from June through August in its outdoor theater. Listening to the music under the stars, whether it be opera, musical comedy or a band from Dublin, San Juan or Chicago, can be a delightful experience. For Summerstage information, call (212) 360-2756.

The place itself is named after the sister of W. Averell Harriman, the wealthy political figure and diplomat who served as governor of New York State from 1955 to 1959. In 1936, when the Casino was demolished (page 40), Mrs. Rumsey donated the money for the children's playground that replaced it. Poorly located for nannies and tots, it was so little used that it was replaced by an open playfield for older children in the 1980s. A few years later, Summerstage moved from the Naumburg Bandshell and established itself at Rumsey.

Outside the entrance of the playfield is an interesting granite statue, *Mother Goose*. Sculpted by F.G.R. Roth, it shows the fictional source of nursery rhymes flying on the back of

a goose. A close look around the sides of the statue reveals carved depictions of Little Jack Horner, Humpty Dumpty and Little Bo Peep. Two smaller statues called *Snow Babies* are perched on either side of the entrance. Playful works in stone by Victor Frisch, they show two small children with their sleds.

Bethesda Terrace

A work of public art that somehow combines grandeur and accessibility, the split-level Bethesda Terrace is the architectural heart of Central Park. At the north end of the Mall, facing the Lake and the wooded Ramble beyond, it offers one of the most scenic views to be found in the middle of a great American city.

Like the Mall, the Terrace has been from the start a place favored by park-fanciers and casual visitors alike. In the 1980s it was given a thorough cleaning and renovation, and today it seems more people-friendly than ever. A prized backdrop for fashion photographers and their models in the quiet morning hours, it is a playground and theater for remarkably diverse crowds on weekends when the weather is fine. As the guiding spirit behind the creation of the Terrace, Calvert Vaux would have been pleased by its popularity. In addition to his strongly held esthetic views, he believed the park was a place to bring people of all classes together. One of his aims, he said, was to "translate Democratic ideas into Trees & Dirt."

Building the Terrace

Vaux also translated his ideas into stone. Doing successful battle with cost-conscious park commissioners, he was able to face nearly all of its railings, posts, staircases, and arches with expensive New Brunswick sandstone. Insisting on the highest standards, he placed responsibility for ornamentation in the hands of Jacob Wrey Mould (page 44), whose decorative genius is apparent almost everywhere in the stonework on both Terrace levels.

On the upper level, which can be reached from the Mall or via the 72nd Street roadway, Vaux created a splendid rectangular concourse. It

A cool and restful retreat since the earliest days of the park, the Wisteria Pergola overlooks the Mall on the northeast side above the Naumberg Bandshell.

The Casino

It is almost forgotten now that the park once had a swinging nightclub. Never a gambling estabishment despite the name, the Casino was located between the Mall and Fifth Avenue in the area now occupied by the Rumsey Playfield.

Designed by Calvert Vaux and opened in 1864 as a Ladies Refreshment House, it began as a two-room stone cottage where food was served at modest cost. But as the decades unfolded, the place became so popular with both sexes that additions were made to the building, prices were hiked and it came to be known as the Casino. In 1928, it was taken over and transformed into a high-priced restaurant and nightspot by cronies of Mayor James J. Walker.

Under its new regime, the Casino catered to the rich and famous. Met at the door by liveried footmen, guests dined on elegant French cuisine, and—despite Prohibition—happily paid inflated prices for mixers to go with the bootleg liquor they brought with them. Dancing, in a spectacular black-glass ballroom to the tunes of Leo Reisman's society orchestra, went on until 3 a.m. Mayor Walker and his mistress, the Broadway showgirl Betty Compton, were often the last to leave.

Not even the stock market crash of October 1929 put an immediate end to the partying. But as the Depression deepened in the early 1930s, many New Yorkers came to see the Casino as a symbol of self-indulgence by privileged people somehow immune to the general hardship. Reform politician Fiorello La Guardia denounced it as a "whoopee joint," and when he was elected mayor at the head of a Republican and Fusion ticket in 1933, the end was in sight for the Casino. In 1935, Parks Commissioner Moses had it torn down and replaced by the Rumsey Playground. Former Mayor Walker, it was said, left a large unpaid bill.

The grand ballroom of the Casino and a Playbill from the mid-1930s

provides a sweeping view of the lower Terrace, the Bethesda Fountain, the Lake and the Ramble. It is also an excellent place for photos. On either side of the concourse, wide stone stairways lead down to the lakeside level.

Vaux also provided direct access to the lower Terrace from the northern terminus of the Mall. Here visitors find a wide flight of stairs flanked by two elaborately carved stone posts, one on the east with images of Day, one on the west with symbols of Night. The stairs descend beneath the driveway to the Arcade, a columned passageway walled by blind bays adorned with trompe l'oeil paintings of recent vintage. The Arcade's chief visual feature, its celebrated ceiling of Minton tiles, is currently undergoing restoration.

The Arcade ends at a row of seven arches opening onto the lower Terrace, an expansive lakeside space with colorful tiles underfoot, low walls of pierced stonework on the periphery and lofty gonfalons snapping in the breeze. On its southern edge are the two massive stone staircases that connect with the upper Terrace. Make a point of walking up or down both stairways for a close look at Mould's beautiful ornamentation depicting fauna and flora of the different seasons.

Bethesda Fountain

At the center of the lower Terrace stands the famous fountain, topped by the winged *Angel of the Waters*, a gilded bronze statue by Emma Stebbins. The symbolism she used in this work reflects a significant event in New York City's history.

The fountain is fed by water from the Croton Aqueduct, opened in 1842. According to the Conservancy's Dennis Burton, "prior to the Croton system city water was plagued by infectious diseases brought on by the overburdened aquifer below Manhattan Island." In the Gospel of John, an angel was said to have "troubled" the pool of Bethesda in Jerusalem and thereby bestowed healing power on its waters. Stebbins felt that the newly acquired gift of clean and wholesome water was worth commemorating.

Beneath the bronze angel she grouped four cherubs representing the Victorian sentiments of Purity, Health, Peace and Temperance. When weather conditions permit, the fountain produces a cloud-like mist that makes the angel appear to be hovering in air as she descends to bestow the gift of healing.

Since its unveiling in 1873, the statue has had its share of critics, with some finding the figure clumsily executed, partially masculine in appearance. To many people, however, the angel was the most memorable feature of the Terrace. They called it the Bethesda Terrace, and the name has stuck.

Curiously enough, when Olmsted and Vaux began to devise their plan for Central Park, they at first considered a terrace near the lake to be "not absolutely necessary." Both believed that buildings should be kept to the minimum. "Nature first, 2nd and 3rd—architecture after a while," wrote Vaux. But as the plan evolved, the partners became convinced that a terrace would "add much to the general effect." Since Vaux was an architect, he naturally assumed that a successful outcome would depend chiefly on his vision and skill. Though neither he nor Olmsted ever took credit publicly for particular aspects of the park plan, in private Vaux described the design of the Terrace as "an original conception of my own in its entirety."

To the dismay of the park commissioners at the time, converting Vaux's ideas into reality proved expensive. But he was determined to construct a terrace that "would let the New Yorker feel that the richest man in New York or elsewhere cannot spend as freely as is here spent just for his lounge." Reluctantly, the commissioners conceded that some "extravagance" would be acceptable.

Largely completed in 1864, the Terrace was highly praised by critics, who compared it favorably to the recently completed Houses of Parliament in London. It also became an immediate hit with the public. They loved the waterside plaza and the nearby boathouse, which rented a variety of conveyances for a tour of the Lake.

Another popular spot was the upper level Terrace. Crowds would gather there each afternoon around four o'clock to watch the carriage parade of finely dressed bigwigs or beautiful young women in their elegant broughams, landaus and victorias. Since they rode across the 72nd Street driveway, the Terrace was "the best place to view the array of horseflesh and vehicles" as well as the "display of beauty and fashion."

With the exception of the clothing of the park visitors, this panoramic view of Bethesda Terrace, published in 1902, looks remarkably similar to its appearance today. Through an ambitious renovation program launched in 1983, the Terrace has been restored to its former glory.

Automobiles put an end to all that, but the Terrace, and particularly the area around Bethesda Fountain, remained a favorite gathering and people-watching place over the years. In the 1960s, however, the scene at the fountain threatened to get out of hand. With scant discouragement from permissive city governments, crowds of young people gathered there to smoke marijuana, play guitars, have an occasional bit of sex and generally "let it all hang out."

Fashion designers came to see the latest variations in jeans, shoes, hats or sunglasses and to filch an idea or two. An article in *Newsweek* called it "Freak Fountain," and described it as the "craziest, gayest, gathering place in the city."

Restoration of the Terrace

Uninhibited conduct, combined with a fiscal crisis in the 1970s that short-changed maintenance, left the Terrace in a sorry state. Surfaces were scarred with graffiti and priceless stone carvings were mutilated. The fountain, usually dry, had become a receptacle for beer cans and other litter. Water seepage had loosened tiles and rusted the gilt ironwork in the Arcade. Frost had damaged flagstones and staircases. The slopes near the Terrace were bare of grass.

New faces in City Hall, improved finances, and changes in attitude toward the park started the Terrace—and the rest of the park— on the road to recovery in the 1980s. In 1983, a four-year restoration program was begun by the Parks Department and the newly-formed Central Park Conservancy. Much of the area around the Terrace was fenced off for a time. Huge sections of ornamented stone balustrades and staircases were hoisted by cranes and taken away for repair. Master stone workers, working with historic photographs, sculpted missing elements and fastened their work to the original surface with steel pins and state-of-the-art adhesive.

Much other mending and cleaning went on. To prevent further water seepage at the Arcade, a new concrete deck was laid under the driveway above. The ceiling, including 16,000 original Minton tiles, was removed for restoration. Damaged sections of the fountain were repaired with bluestone from the original quarry and steps on the stairways had to be reset. The maltreated knolls nearby were freshly landscaped with grass and flowering shrubs including rhododendrons and azaleas.

By the end of the 1980s, the entire Terrace area looked enormously better. All told, the renovation had cost

Believed to be the most photographed monument in the park, the bronze sculpture, Angel of the Waters, designed by Emma Stebbins, symbolizes the purifying of the city's water supply brought about by the opening of the Croton Aqueduct in 1842.

Jacob Wrey Mould

A Designer Extraordinaire of Bethesda Terrace

Among the makers of Central Park, only Olmsted and Vaux eclipsed Jacob Wrey Mould. Little remembered now, he was regarded by his peers in mid-19th century America as a remarkably gifted architect with a genius for ornamentation. As Vaux's assistant, he brought a special touch to many of the park's buildings. It is still visible in the park today and still a source of delight, particularly in the decorative artistry at the Terrace.

But Mould, an unconventional personality, was viewed with distaste by some of his contemporaries. Like Vaux, he was an Englishman, but where Vaux was modest, Mould was flamboyant and boastful. He borrowed money frequently and paid it back slowly. In a conservative society, he shocked many by living openly with a woman without the benefit of wedlock. George Templeton Strong, a prominent New Yorker and one of Mould's creditors, dipped his pen in acid to describe Mould in his diary as "that ugly and uncouth but very clever J. Wrey Mould architect and universal genius."

Although this judgment may be tinged with sarcasm, Strong was perfectly aware of Mould's superb artistic ability and training. As a promising young man, he was apprenticed to Owen Jones, and spent years in Spain helping the eminent English architect prepare a study of the Alhambra and the authoritative *Grammar of Ornament*. Judging by Mould's later work, he was indelibly influenced by the spirit of Moorish art and architecture.

In 1853, Mould emigrated to New York, where he quickly established himself as a designer of churches, schools and private homes. He became acquainted with Vaux and Olmsted, assisted them in crafting their plan for Central Park, and became Vaux's assistant when they were chosen to build it. In that capacity, he helped to design many park structures, including the Dairy, the Belvedere and many of the arches and bridges.

Skilled with metal as well as brick and stone, Mould was the sole designer of the gaily decorated cast-iron bandstand that once graced the Mall area and the Ladies

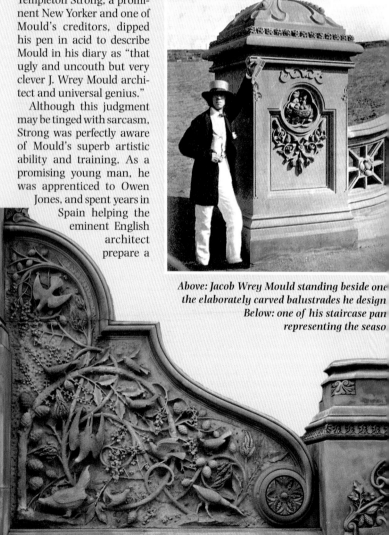

Above: Jacob Wrey Mould standing beside one
the elaborately carved balustrades he design
Below: one of his staircase pan
representing the seaso

Pavillion that stands today at Hernshead on the west shore of the lake. Mould also designed the brick and stone Sheepfold that now houses the Tavern on the Green.

But by far the greatest contribution Mould made to the park can be seen at the Terrace. While Vaux provided its overall architecture, Mould created the beautiful, often ingenious ornamentation. On the upper level, at the north end of the Mall, he embellished the posts and railings of the sandstone screen walls with a rich variety of stylized leaves and berries. His reliefs on the posts flanking the stairway down to the Arcade and the lakeside Terrace are delightful.

In the Arcade under the drive, Mould covered the ceiling with brilliantly colorful tiles that he designed and had made by the Minton Company in England. To prevent them from coming loose and falling, he anchored them to the ceiling in a lattice of gilded ironwork, creating what a contemporary called "an underground jewell box."

Perhaps Mould's most extraordinary work can be found on the two stone staircases leading from the upper level to the Bethesda Fountain plaza. On either side of each massively balustraded stairway are intricately fashioned arabesques depicting the seasons, each uniquely vibrant with birds, insects and plant life. When he inspected these reliefs shortly after the park's opening, art critic Clarence Cook wrote that "on no public building in America has there yet been placed any sculpture so rich in design as this, or so exquisitely delicate in execution."

When Mould died in 1886, an acquaintance wrote that "he died almost friendless I learn, although the woman he called his wife stuck to him to the last." But if he was an uncomfortably free spirit for many in his time, Mould's uncommon gifts and his exceptional work won him the admiration of peers like Olmsted and Vaux. A glance at what remains of his distinctive achievement tells us that it was an enormous stroke of luck that the singular Jacob Wrey Mould lived in New York when one of the world's greatest parks was being created.

the city and Conservancy $7.8 million. But most park lovers would agree that it was well worth the money and effort.

On any given day, thousands of students, tourists and everyday New Yorkers can be seen inspecting the stonework, admiring the lakeside view or taking pictures of the fountain. The statue of the *Angel of the Waters* is said to be the most photographed object in Central Park. Some visitors come just to sit at the edge of the Terrace and gaze with admiration at Calvert Vaux's beautifully restored masterpiece. "Of all I have ever done," he said, "it is perhaps the only thing that gives me much encouragement that I have in me the germ of an architect." Vaux, as was his custom, was being far too modest.

Singer Lilac Walk

If the sight and scent of lilacs in the spring tickle your fancy, then the Singer Lilac Walk should be on your agenda. An ordinary-looking cinder path along the northeast edge of the Sheep Meadow in the winter months, it is transformed into a fragrant wonderland of purple, pink and white lilac blossoms in April, May and early June.

At these peak times, on one side of the walk the meadow's fence is covered with morning glories and clematis; behind the fence a line of lilac and fruit trees offers a palette of delicate blooms. But it is the lawn on the other side of the walk that holds the special treasure of the place, a gloriously thick, artfully composed cluster of lilac bushes and lilac trees. The mix of bloom times and blossom colors, and of common and hybrid varieties, is expertly designed by park gardeners for the greatest visual effect.

Since colonial days, the traditional common lilac has been a favorite flowering shrub in America. Among the common lilacs (*Syringa vulgaris*) along the walk are Dutch, Southeast European and American varieties. One of the latter is the splendid "President Lincoln," which blooms in April and inevitably recalls Walt Whitman's great elegy for Lincoln, "When Lilacs Last in the Dooryard Bloom'd."

Other unique varieties are the "Nocturne" and "MacFarlane" from Canada, the "Miss Kim," "Katherine Havermeyer," and "Annual" from the United States, and a beautiful nameless pink lilac from China. Adding variation in form and color are hybrids from the U.S. and France. The hybrids, which often lack the fragrance of common lilacs, are sometimes called French lilacs in honor of the pioneering work on hybridizing done in France.

The Lilac Walk was the idea of philanthropist Nell Singer, whose gift financed its creation in 1970. During the years 1990 and 1991, Conservancy gardeners carried out

The Lilac Walk is a wonderland of white, pink and purple blossoms in the spring. Among them are eleven varieties, from the U.S., Canada, Europe and China.

a major replanting of the beds, which since have been treated with exceptional care. As a result, the little path along the Sheep Meadow is a place to which many park lovers are drawn when the lilacs burst into flower each spring.

The Sheep Meadow

A luxuriant expanse of grass on the west side of the park in the mid-60s, the Sheep Meadow is a popular place these days for sunbathing, frisbee tossing, and other innocent urban pastimes. The turmoil and dispute that surrounded this gently rolling greensward over the years seem forgotten. And long gone are the sheep that once grazed here and spent their nights across the West Drive in the Sheepfold, whose admirable building now houses the Tavern on the Green.

No matter how warm the month of March may be, the Parks Department waits until mid-April every year to reopen the Sheep Meadow. Only then will the sod have recovered from the previous season and be strong enough to withstand new hordes of people. On a typical day, 30,000 people may come. A good time for a walk through the meadow is on a weekday, soon after opening time of 11 a.m. With few people

about, a ramble through the grassy fifteen-acre tract ringed by sturdy oak, elm, maple and plane trees can be a refreshing experience. Adding an almost dreamlike quality is a panoramic view of the Manhattan skyline.

On weekends during fine weather, the ambience is far different. Radio playing, team sports and "dogs, on or off leash" are banned, and many people are quietly reading, tanning or people-watching. But all is not tranquil. Frisbees and occasionally footballs whizz through the air. Kites unpredictably dive to earth, sometimes disturbingly close to the unwary. Should these activities grow too noisy or the sound of an illicit boom-box be heard, offenders are reminded of the sign stating that the "area is reserved for quiet enjoyment."

The proper use of this site has been debated since the inception of the park. A place for military drilling had been required by the design competition for Central Park. So Olmsted and Vaux, in their prize-winning plan, located a "Parade Ground" on the area now occupied by the meadow. But they and the early park comissioners, fearing that a military presence would attract unruly crowds, strongly objected to such activities in the park. They began referring to the area as "the Green" in official documents, and they resisted its use by the military, even during the Civil War. Around 1864, they emphasized their point by introducing a large flock of Southdown sheep, and after a few years the public came to call the place the Sheep Meadow. In 1870, a Sheepfold was built across the drive, and twice a day a shepherd would hold up carriage traffic, and later automobiles, as he drove the animals to and from the meadow.

For some decades, access to the meadow was severely restricted. The general public was allowed in only on Sundays. But by the 1910s and 1920s, city governments had grown more permissive. As preservationists shuddered, large historical pageants, as well as athletic and patriotic events, were held on the lawn. In 1912, a crowd of 30,000 watched as 5000 schoolchildren performed in a pageant called "Around the World in Search of Fairyland." The spectacle was illuminated by 10,000 red, white and blue lights.

Through all this, the sheep continued to lend a pastoral touch, but in 1934 the innovating parks commissioner Robert Moses deemed them unsightly and exiled the flock to Prospect Park in Brooklyn. There they remained for a short while before disappearing into history. The shepherd was given a job at the Lion House in the Zoo. Fortunately, the Sheepfold was preserved and transformed into the restaurant called Tavern on the Green.

The meadow itself was kept in good condition until the 1960s, when park authorities permitted a series of concerts and rallies that attracted massive crowds. In 1967, during a huge protest against the Vietnam War, demonstrators shredded draft cards, burned American flags and mutilated the grass and shrubs. In 1969, thousands marched from Greenwich Village to hold a "gay-in" at the Sheep Meadow. At a hippie "love-in" that year, participants fought with police and built a bonfire with tree branches and barricades; one young man was badly burned when he stripped and threw himself into the fire.

Between the behavior of the crowds and a fiscally troubled city's neglect, the turf eventually was destroyed and the soil compacted. By the mid-1970s the Sheep Meadow, more brown than green, had become a dust bowl. But changes at City Hall and improved finances enabled a determined new team of park leaders to call a halt to its decline and begin its renascence. In 1979, the meadow was totally resodded, and in the early 1980s the Central Park Conservancy took control of much of the park's maintenance and enhancement. The Sheep Meadow was surrounded by a chain-link fence, strict new rules of personal conduct were enforced, and large-scale public events were tabooed.

The improvement has been startling. Expert care has been lavished on the Sheep Meadow and today it is

Sheep grazed in the park until the 1930s when Commissioner Moses banned them, supposedly because they were inbred and producing abnormal lambs.

An architectural treasure, the Sheepfold housed the sheep and shepherd until 1934, when it was transformed into the Tavern on the Green restaurant.

immaculate and beautiful. Its magnificent open green space and spectacular view have been reclaimed for New Yorkers and visitors alike.

The Sheepfold

One of the park's lesser-known architectural treasures, the Sheepfold is today concealed within the elaborate layout of the Tavern on the Green. The sprightly brick and stone structure, designed by Jacob Wrey Mould, is considered an outstanding example of mid-Victorian architecture of the cottage type.

The Sheepfold was built in 1870 to house the flock that grazed across the road and its shepherd. But though its purpose was utilitarian, Mould did not suppress his characteristic ingenuity and flair. As described by Olmsted and Vaux, the low-slung, semicircular structure had a "high pitched, slate roof, decorated with turrets and gilded iron work" and walls "of pressed brick, with trimmings of cut blue stone and polished granite." It also included a series of elegant gabled doorways embellished with decorative tiles and ornate stonework.

Changes have been made over the years. Some of the turrets have been removed. A glass-enclosed dining room swells into what once was the Sheepfold's front yard. But the building's exterior remains largely intact. For the best look, walk along the bridle path on its east side. If the garden areas of the restaurant are not busy, for instance in the late morning

The Geology of the Park

Newcomers to the park are sometimes surprised by the number of large rocky outcroppings scattered across much of the landscape. What are those dark rocks? How old are they? How did they get those shapes and markings? The curiosity is warranted, since the park does have an unusually rich endowment of exposed ancient bedrock. The rocks are not only highly decorative; they also contain visible evidence of epochal events dating back hundreds of millions of years.

For some insight into that deep history, a good place to explore is the massive outcropping on the western edge of the Heckscher Playground in the lower park. Called the Umpire Rock, perhaps because it has a commanding view of the baseball diamonds nearby, it is almost entirely composed of Manhattan schist. This is an extremely durable, mica-flecked stone that comprises 90 percent of the bedrock under Manhattan Island and underlies nearly all of Central Park. The schist was formed from sedimentary shale by intense subterranean heat and pressure some 450 million years ago in the Paleozoic Era.

An even older formation, a softer rock called Inwood marble, is found only in the extreme north of the park. The oldest of the three layers making up the foundation of New York City is Fordham gneiss, which underlies the other two and may date back over a billion years. It surfaces primarily in the Bronx and not at all in Central Park.

While the schist of the Umpire Rock was being formed, it was twisted and folded by upheavals in the earth's depths. Minerals scattered in the former shale were fused into crystals of quartz, mica, feldspar and garnet within the schist. It later underwent other alterations, as an inspection of its

before lunch, it is usually permissible to enter and inspect the Sheepfold at close hand. In its setting amid the restaurant's theatrical topiary and Japanese lanterns, Mould's imaginative dwelling for sheep more than holds its own.

Tavern on the Green

The largest and most popular full-scale restaurant in Central Park, the renowned Tavern on the Green serves upward of half a million people every year. Festive and convivial, the glittering establishment on the western edge of the park at 67th Street is expert at providing fantasy as well as an eclectic, pricey range of dishes.

Since its opening in 1934, the restaurant has undergone a number of renovations, growing more and more dazzling with each. Glass-

Glacial striations can clearly be seen on Umpire Rock located adjacent to the Heckscher Playground.

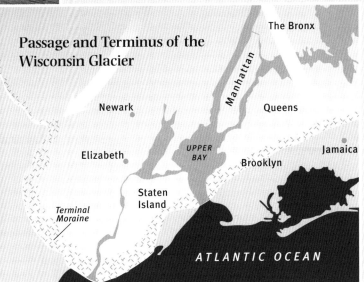

Passage and Terminus of the Wisconsin Glacier

The Bronx

Manhattan

Newark

Queens

Elizabeth

UPPER BAY

Jamaica

Brooklyn

Staten Island

Terminal Moraine

ATLANTIC OCEAN

surface will attest. Lighter-colored veins of granite and coarser granite pegmatite intrude across the grain into the body of the host rock. These inlays once were liquified rock in the inferno of the earth's interior before being injected into fissures in the schist and cooling into bands of solid rock.

Other traces of the Umpire Rock's eventful past were left by the glacier of the most recent Ice Age. The ponderous mass spread south from the Arctic and eventually came to rest where New York City stands today, covering it in a thousand-foot thickness of ice around 30,000 years ago. The abrasive action of gravel, sand, rock fragments and boulders carried along by the glacier scoured the surfaces of the exposed bedrock. Clearly visible on the Umpire Rock are a shiny glacial polish, many aligned scratches called "striations," and deeply gouged grooves, some creating giant fingers of stone.

Other major outcroppings in the park of course share much of the Umpire Rock's geological history and show comparable glacial sculpting. The various parts of the park also share other souvenirs left behind by the glacier. When it melted and retreated about 11,000 years ago, it left behind a good deal of sand, gravel and clay, much of which is still present in the earth surrounding or covering the bedrock. It also deposited many rocks and boulders, called "erratics" because they are not native to the area, randomly across the park site.

One especially interesting erratic is a boldly striped rock of gneiss secluded along the shoreline of the Ramble across the Lake from the Terrace. Probably torn from the Ramapo Mountains to the northwest, the rock is old enough to inspire a sense of awe. Some geologists believe it dates back well over a billion years.

enclosed rooms were added to the Victorian-era building it inherited from the old Sheepfold. Its halls and dining areas are now crammed with paintings, antique prints, etched mirrors, Tiffany glass and crystal chandeliers. The outdoor dining areas are something to behold. Large topiary animals, including a reindeer, an elephant and a gorilla inhabit the greenery. Hundreds of lanterns and thousands of tiny lights are everywhere, in the trees and bushes, on the sculpted animals and along the lines of the building.

At night, only the most determined grouches would deny that the Tavern on the Green takes on a delightful, romantic air. The food? The quality varies from year to year, but for most visitors, that is probably a secondary concern.

SOUTH CENTRAL QUADRANT
73rd Street to 85th Street

Map

Playground

84 St. — M10

RO PIN

SCALE
One city block
(north to south)
equals approxima
1/20th of a mile
1/13th of a kilom

83 St.

Summit Rock

82 St.

Diana Ross Playground

Winterdale Arch

De

81 St. — Hunters' Gate

B,C

Urban Park Rangers

Swedish Cottage Marionette Theatre

American Museum of Natural History

Maintenance Yard

Shakespea Gard

M10

Bow Bridge

W E S T

Alexander von Humboldt

Bank Rock Bridge

Rust Ston Arch

77 St. — M10
New York Historical Society

Explorers' Gate

Balcony Bridge

EAST DRIVE

76 St.

HERNSHEAD

Bri No

75 St. — M10

Ladies Pavilion

C E N T R A L   P A R K

74 St.

THE LAKE

N

73 St.

STRAWBERRY FIELDS

Womens' Gate

72 St. — M10

B,C

Wisteria Arbors

Wisteria Arbor

Wagne Cove

Riftstone Arch

"Imagine" mosaic

Daniel Webster

71 St.

70 St.

Fal

MAP CONTINUED ON PAGE 1

Legend

TRANSVERSES — ROADWAYS — BRIDLE PATHS

POLICE CALL BOX — INFORMATION DESK — PUBLIC PHONE — FOOD SERVICE — POLICE STATION — RE ROO

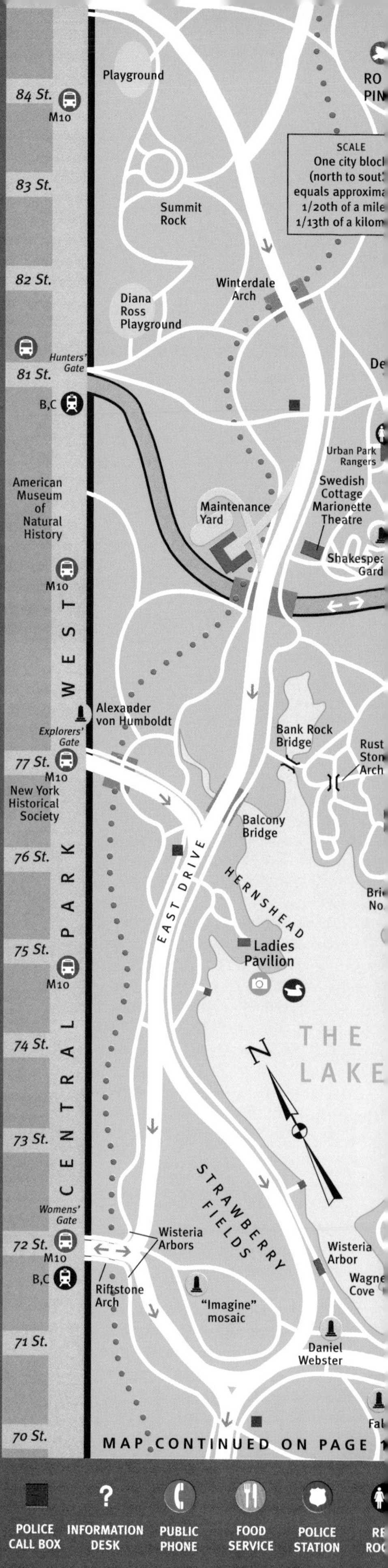

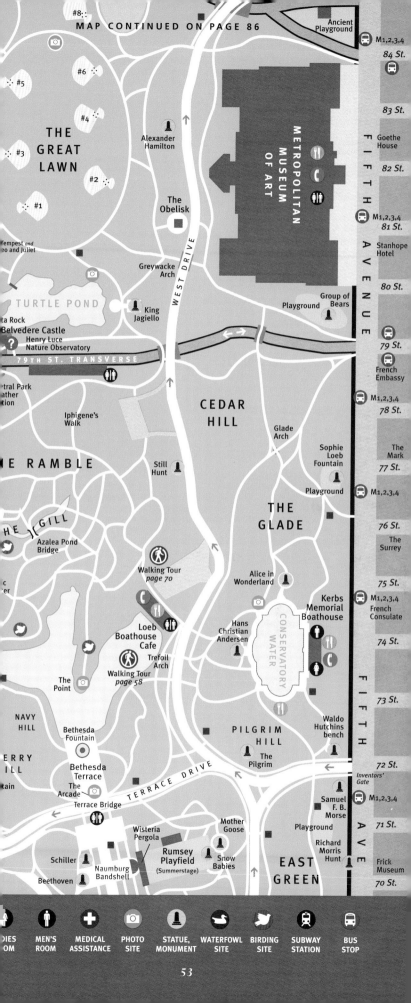

Conservatory Water

"Civilized" may be the word for the area of the park around the little body of water officially called the Conservatory Water. Located just north of the entrance at 72nd Street at Fifth Avenue, it is only blocks from one of the busiest neighborhoods on the Upper East Side. Yet its natural beauty, delightful statuary, and amenities for children as well as adults, have made it an extremely pleasant place to stop for a refreshment and watch the passing scene.

Although fishing is not permitted, it is not unusual to see small children furtively dangling lines over the pond's edge. This may be yet another triumph of hope over experience. Small aquatic creatures such as crayfish, goldfish, and even jellyfish have been known to find their way into the pond through the inflow pipe. But few pond-watchers have ever seen anything other than a paper cup fished out of the Conservatory Water.

Why, you may ask, does such a charm-

Above: Fifth Avenue apartment buildings reflected in the Conservatory Water. Below: Model boat yachtsmen dressed in their Sunday best in the 1920s.

ing little pond have such an imposing name? Because originally it was
supposed to adjoin a large iron and
glass conservatory, or greenhouse,
for the display of plants. The building was never constructed because
of financial problems, but the pond
was created and over the decades it
has been used for ice skating, the
Gaelic sport of curling, and for sail-
ing model boats.

Kerbs Memorial Boathouse

The Conservatory Water itself is
usually called the boat pond or sailboat pond, and for good reason. On
most pleasant days, a variety of
model ships, most of them remote-
controlled, glide and tack on the
water as their skippers watch proudly from the rim. The sailboats are
either privately owned or rented at a
cart provided by the nearby Kerbs
Memorial Boathouse. The more avid
aficionados can apply for permits to
stow their ships there.

On Saturdays, starting around
10:00 a.m. races are held, with participants ranging from youngsters in
backwards caps to cigar chomping
veterans. How many of them are
aware that Stuart Little, the mouse in
E. B. White's classic children's story,
sailed his fictional sailboat to victory
many years ago on this very pond?

In 1954, an old wooden boathouse was replaced by the current
one, a red brick building with a
jaunty copper roof and steeple.
Inside are row after row of model
ships, some quite impressive, which
visitors are allowed to admire from
a distance.

Outside the boathouse is a handsome flagstone patio, where benches
and tables offer a respite to weary
sightseers, early morning joggers,
and park habitues in flight from the
city streets. Light food and drink are
available at the counter next to the
boathouse and an ice cream stand at
the south end of the pond. Weather
permitting, it is a most agreeable
place to sit under overhanging
branches and watch the sailboats,
read a paper or eavesdrop on conver-
sations in a multitude of languages.
People with small children seem
delighted to find a clean, attractive
sandbox at one end of the patio.

At times, the scene on the promenade around the pond takes on a festive atmosphere. Violinists and
accordionists play old European
airs. Jugglers and clowns appear and
find appreciative audiences. Most
interesting of all to many visitors
are the hawk watchers, who station
themselves and their high-powered
telescopes along the southwest rim

of the pond on most weekends. They come to keep close watch over the red-tailed hawks that have been nesting on a ledge above a 12th-floor window of a building on Fifth Avenue, and they happily offer passers-by a close-up view.

The fact that the building in question is inhabited by Mary Tyler Moore, or that Woody Allen sometimes appears on a balcony next door, is of little consequence to the hawk watchers. They are concerned about the mating of the hawks, and the hatching of the eggs, and forays of both hawk parents into the park to catch pigeons or rats for themselves and their new brood. Marie Winn, a hawk watcher and author of *Red-Tails in Love: A Wildlife Drama in Central Park*, says that watching the human celebrities is not very exciting: "It's not like someone coming back with a rat and feeding babies."

By the end of May or early June, the young birds make their fledgling flights, flapping out of the nest for brief sorties over the park and back. The hawk watchers are ecstatic. This, say the Central Park Rangers, may be the first successful red-tailed hawk nest in Manhattan since the 19th century. Evidently the raptors find their spot on Fifth Avenue satis-factory, since 1998 was the fourth year in a row they raised their young at that address.

Far different attractions along the pathway around the pond are the vastly appealing statues of Hans Christian Andersen and *Alice in Wonderland*. Both are high on the list of stops for many visitors, especially those with children, and both are popular sites for snapping pictures.

Hans Christian Andersen

The bronze of Andersen, on the west side of the pond, has the Danish writer of 168 fairy tales sitting on a bench with an open volume whose pages are turned to the story of *The Ugly Duckling*. At his feet, a bronze duck seems to be paying him close attention. It is easy for children to climb onto Andersen's lap, which many of them do, to the delight of their parents. The statue, sculpted by Chicago-born Georg Lober and given to the park by the Danish-American Women's Association, was installed in 1956 and has been a favorite ever since. On summer weekends, storytellers stand before the statue and hold their mixed-generation audiences spellbound with lively renditions of Andersen's stories and folktales from around the world.

A favorite spot for children, the Hans Christian Andersen statue commemorates the famous Danish author and his best known book **The Ugly Duckling.**

Alice in Wonderland

A short stroll to the northern edge of the pond takes visitors to perhaps the most popular piece of statuary in the park, the *Alice in Wonderland* group. Alice is shown sitting on a large mushroom surrounded by many of the characters in Lewis Carroll's fantasy world, including the Mad Hatter, the March Hare, the White Rabbit, the Dormouse, the Cheshire Cat, the Caterpillar and Alice's kitten, Dinah. The face of the Mad Hatter is said to be a caricature of George Delacorte, who donated the statue in memory of his wife. The many irregular surfaces of the eleven-foot-high work seem to invite children to climb all over it, and they have done so over the years, polishing the bronze to a golden finish. Sculpted by Spanish-born José de Creeft, Alice was unveiled in 1959 and since has delighted park visitors from all over the world.

The Conservatory Water and its environs have so many points of interest that it is easy to take the admirable natural setting for granted. The gently undulating grassy slopes around the pond are virtually a showcase for a stunning variety of trees. Widely spaced, they have developed exceptionally well-shaped foliage. North and west of the pond stand many towering London plane trees, a robust hybrid found in many areas of the park, and a scattering of willows, pines and beeches. The area south of the pond includes nine varieties of oak, a few black cherries and some Lebanon cedars, a Levantine species rarely found this far north. Near the ice cream stand are splendid examples of the Norway maple and the related Schwedler Norway maple, whose leaves are purple-red in the spring before fading to green during the summer.

In the spring, the grounds around the pond are in their glory. Cherry trees on the north and west of the pond are hung with pink and white blossoms. The mulberry bushes in front of the boathouse are bedecked with white flowers. Hosts of golden daffodils glow everywhere on the sunshiny green lawns and on the slopes leading up to Pilgrim Hill.

Pilgrim Hill

This little knoll, which rises to the southwest of the boat pond, evidently takes its name from the well-known statue on its crest called *The Pilgrim*. Sculpted and caste in bronze by John Quincy Adams Ward, perhaps the leading American sculptor of the immediate post-

At the north end of the sailboat pond is José de Creeft's beloved sculpture of Lewis Carroll's characters from Alice in Wonderland. Alice sits atop a magic toadstool flanked by the March Hare, the Mad Hatter, the Dormouse and Alice's kitten, Dinah.

A gift to the City from the New England Society, the Pilgrim monument by John Quincy Adams Ward was dedicated in 1885 to pay homage to the original Plymouth Rock settlers.

Civil War period, it shows a resolute Pilgrim Father, musket at the ready, prepared to face whatever challenges might arise in the new world of America. On the granite pedestal are four bas-reliefs depicting "Bible and Sword," the ship "Mayflower," "Cross-bow and Arrows," and "Commerce."

The statue, a gift of the *New England Society* in 1884, has its critics, who believe it focuses excessively on the costume and not enough on the character of the man. Some also fault the clumsiness of the pedestal by Richard Morris Hunt. Still, the piece has a certain sturdy simplicity that has earned it many admirers.

But what, one wonders, can be going through the mind of this 17th century settler as he looks sternly down at a 72nd Street crossway bustling with inline skaters, bare-legged men and women, and armadas of honking automobiles?

A Tour of the Lake

Perhaps no area of the park has given so much pleasure to so many people over the years as the Lake. Spreading across 20 acres north of the 72nd Street driveway, it is the largest accessible body of water in the park and by far the most varied in its physical beauty and recre-

ational attractions. Visitors by the millions come each year to stroll on its banks, row on its gentle waters, or just savor what the park's designers called "scenic refreshment."

Today, the Lake and its peripheral areas are more appealing than ever. Viewed from places as diverse as the Bethesda Terrace, the Loeb Boathouse, the Bow Bridge or Hernshead, its many gently curved shorelines, the overhanging trees and the rocky, forested backdrop of the Ramble lend the Lake an almost storybook charm. The skyscrapers and residential towers rising beyond the tree lines to the east and west add an interesting contrast. Little wonder that so many people on the pathways along the water's edge have their cameras at the ready.

On most weekdays, activity on the Lake itself can be minimal. Children fish from jutting rocks, dogs splash into the water to fetch sticks, and squadrons of ducks paddle about. Swans, once numerous, have all but disappeared from the Lake, and by early 1998 only two mature swans were left.

Loeb Boathouse

A handful of rowers are on the water most days, but on weekends they often descend on the Lake in force to form a disorganized flotilla that has been lampooned as the Central Park Navy. Boats can be rented at the Loeb Boathouse, located at the northeastern tip of the Lake, for $10.00 an hour, with a $30.00 cash deposit. Gondola rides for up to six people are available for $30.00 a half hour, with reservations required. Call (212) 517-3623.

Even before the Lake was completely built, it was understood that it would serve as a playground as well as a place for the "visual recreation" emphasized by Olmsted and Vaux. Throughout the summer and fall of 1858, as an army of laborers toiled to create a lake from the south branch of the Sawkill Creek and the marsh it flowed through, newspapers demanded that they finish in time for winter ice skating. While one work gang excavated huge amounts of earth and rock from the bogland and built a terraced shoreline, another laid great drainage pipes to carry water in and out of the area. Work was not yet completed, but on a frigid day in December enough water was let in so that some skating could begin.

After the Lake was completed, ice skating became the rage in New York. When the ice was thick enough, flags with a red ball signaling that fact were displayed on horsecars coming to the park and also from a tower on Vista Rock— now the site of Belvedere Castle. Enormous crowds swarmed into the park in the late 1850s and early 1860s to skate, primarily on the

A popular spot for observing waterfowl, the area of the Lake near Cherry Hill (right) is flanked by the stately arch of Bow Bridge (left). Swans, mallards and blue herons are frequent visitors along the shore.

Lake. Some days the crowds reached from 75,000 to 100,000 people. Skates could be rented for ten cents an hour, and many skated at night by artificial light from calcium reflectors situated along the shoreline.

Part of the Lake, in the far northwest corner, was set aside as a "Ladies Pond," but many women defied the era's conventions of public behavior by skating on the main pond along with the men. Skating must have led to other things, since a guidebook of the time reported that "Many a young fellow has lost his heart, and skated himself into matrimony, on the Central Park pond."

Boating also was popular from the park's earliest days. Rowboats could be hired and two kinds of multi-seated passenger boats were available—water buses that picked up riders at the steps of the Terrace every fifteen minutes for a circuit of the Lake at a cost of ten cents and private "call" boats hired by the hour. Six rustic landings were built around the water's rim to board and discharge passengers. Many people went boating at night, sometimes in a rented gondola complete with an authentic singing Venetian gondolier. At times the boaters, as well as crowds lining the shores, were treated to the music of a brass band playing on a barge out on the Lake. The passenger boats remained in service until the 1920s; four of the landings remain stand-

ing today, in somewhat altered form, at their original locations.

In the 1860s, a number of temporary shack-like buildings served the rowing public as boathouses. The first was located just to the west of

Gondola rides were introduced to the park by Commissioner John A. C. Gray in 1862. These authentic Venetian gondoliers, c.1900, could be hired to pole visitors and their loved ones around the Lake while singing arias from the then popular operas of Puccini and Verdi.

Promenades along the shoreline and boating on the Lake were favorite Sunday pleasures. This 1894 photograph looks west towards the original, ornately carved boathouse.

the Terrace, but in 1873 a long wooden structure designed by Vaux was erected on the eastern shoreline. It provided covered space for docking and storing rowboats and a second-story terrace for viewing the sur-

Women found that ice skating afforded them a sanctioned release from their socially circumscribed behavior. This Currier & Ives print shows that skating was one of the rare activities in which "respectable women" could display their ankles in public.

rounding scenery. A charming building with touches of Victorian ornamentation, it served for over eighty years, but by the 1950s it was seen as a decrepit eyesore, unfit to service a growing number of rowers.

In 1952, the old boathouse was demolished, and two years later the current building—largely financed with a gift from investment banker Carl Loeb—was opened. Located at the northeastern tip of the Lake, the Loeb Boathouse is a functional red brick and limestone complex, topped by a copper roof with an attractive green patina. It holds an airy, well-run cafeteria, a more expensive restaurant with a terrace at the water's edge, and an elegant section set aside for private parties and weddings. A small lakeside cafe and bar serves drinks in an adjoining area. The rowboats? The rental booth and docking ramps can be found a few paces away.

To the northwest of the Boathouse is the Ramble, whose shoreline forms a good part of the Lake's perimeter. (That section of the lakeshore is described on page 70.) But for a walking tour of the many other points of interest along the borders of the Lake, visitors might start at the boathouse and head south along the east shore. The walkway passes Trefoil Arch on the left and soon arrives at Bethesda Terrace (page 39). Situated at the edge of the water, this superb plaza is an excellent place to pause for a sweeping view of the eastern sector of the Lake and part of the Ramble's rocky, forested shoreline. On quiet days, with luck, it is also a good spot to watch the stilt-legged egrets that sometimes come to hunt for fish and frogs among the nearby reeds. At the northwest corner of the Terrace is a pathway that leads north along a pretty stretch of lakeside and, after a short distance, to the Bow Bridge.

Bow Bridge

One of the most beautiful small bridges in the world, it was designed by Calvert Vaux and Jacob Wrey Mould, and its construction was completed in 1862. The uncommonly graceful sweep of its cast-iron span and the lavish ornamentation of its 142-foot balustrade have made it one of the most admired objects in the park.

Renovated in 1998, the bridge was given a new wood walkway made of ipe, a South American hardwood, and painted ivory and beige to replicate the original colors. The center of the bridge provides a panoramic view, much favored by bird watchers

Designed by Calvert Vaux and Jacob Wrey Mould, Bow Bridge is visible from the water's edge next to a rustic boat landing. Completed in 1862, this graceful cast-iron span is exquisitely detailed with Gothic quatrefoils, abstract foliage and interlaced spirals. Large vases overflowing with flowering plants (inset) originally graced the four corners. The bridge has recently been restored and repainted in its original colors.

during the spring and fall migrations. It is also an excellent place to view and photograph the skylines on Fifth Avenue and Central Park West and to watch the rowboats and their wonderfully assorted occupants pass from one side of the Lake to the other.

Cherry Hill

Continuing along the path heading southwest, a stroller has a wonderful view of the Bow Bridge, the little reed-choked island to its west and a wide expanse of the western lobe of the Lake and shoreline. On the left a lawn area often frequented by sunbathers and picnickers leads up a gentle slope to Cherry Hill. The name derives from the many nearby cherry trees that flaunt their pink and white blossoms each springtime.

On the crest of the hill is a circular concourse, a popular gathering spot in the 19th century for people on horseback or in carriages. There they rested, gossiped and watered the animals at the fountain, a whimsical Victorian horse trough created most probably by Mould. The water flows out of eight little flowers into a circle of bowls, then spills down onto a rounded granite skirt before dripping lightly into the pool.

Ornamental tiles, multi-colored stone, and a black and gilt cast-iron structure topped by eight round lamps and a golden spire complete the picture. The fountain had not been operative for years until August 1998, when a restoration project by the Conservancy cleaned it up, gave it a bright new paint job and got the water flowing again. Today, horse-drawn carriages rented on 59th Street clatter up to Cherry Hill, just as others did in the early days of the park. But times have changed, even for horses. Now they are not allowed to drink from what was once their own watering fountain.

A visit to Cherry Hill in the spring and early summer is particularly rewarding when the forsythia and, later, the multi-colored flowering azaleas are in bloom.

Wagner Cove

Before leaving Cherry Hill, find the stone stairway on the west of the concourse that leads down to a secluded corner of the Lake. This is Wagner Cove, named for Robert Wagner, mayor of New York from 1954 to 1965. It is a strikingly scenic little hideaway, with a bold outcropping of bedrock, many overhanging trees twittering with birds, and a colorful variety of shrubs and flowers. At the edge of the water is a wooden shelter with benches, one of the four landings surviving—in somewhat remodeled form—from the passenger boat days. Just as in the 19th century, this colorful area is popular with artists and photographers, with film makers adding a contemporary touch.

Daniel Webster Statue

Returning to Cherry Hill, take the pathway at its southwest and follow it around the bottom of the cove. Ahead will be an oversized bronze statue of Daniel Webster; the stiff pomposity bestowed on him by sculptor Thomas Ball does little justice to the outstanding 19th century orator and senator from Massachusetts (photo page 125).

During the first generation after Webster's death, former Abolitionists and their sympathizers, remembering Webster's support of the Compromise of 1850, often pictured him as a man whose career had come to ruin because of his character defects. The memoirs of President John Quincy Adams, published in the 1870s, contained a reference to "the gigantic intellect, the envious temper, the ravenous ambition, and the rotten heart of Daniel Webster." Meanwhile, his former intimates recalled him as the "godlike Daniel," a man of irresistible charm as well as surpassing statesmanship. Some writers said his patriotic statements inspired the Union during the Civil War, and even Abraham Lincoln echoed a number of those praises.

It should also be pointed out here

that Daniel was *not* the lexicographer for whom Webster's Dictionary is named. That honor belongs to Noah Webster.

After passing in front of the statue, cross the drive to the west and enter the pathway leading up the slope into Strawberry Fields.

Strawberry Fields

Once a fairly nondescript area stretching from 71st to 74th streets, it was transformed into its present, superbly landscaped condition through a gift from Yoko Ono. She presented Strawberry Fields to the park as a memorial to her husband,

Flowers are often left by visitors at the site of this Italian mosaic memorial in Strawberry Fields to the Beatles' John Lennon.

Looking west toward the shores of Hernshead, a peninsula on the Lake, so named for its rocky contour resembling the head of a heron.

the late singer and composer John Lennon, after his murder in front of the Dakota apartment house on Central Park West in 1980. It was named not only for the Beatles' well-know song, "Strawberry Fields Forever," but also for an orphanage in Liverpool, England where as a child Lennon played with friends who lived there.

Are there any actual strawberries in Strawberry Fields? Well, it seems that plantings of strawberry bushes have not been successful due to a scarcity of sun in this quarter of the park. Only a few scattered bushes are to be found among its rich variety of shrubs including rhododendron, jetbead, sweet pepper, rose and witch hazel. The area also has an impressive variety of robust trees, beautiful lawns and over a hundred species of plants sent as gifts from countries around the world. An official plaque calls the site a "Garden of Peace."

At nearly every season of the year, people come from all over the world to pay homage to Lennon. Many especially seek out a circular black and white mosaic set in a pathway. A gift of the city of Naples, Italy, a single word in its center recalls another one of Lennon's songs: "Imagine."

Returning to the path by the Lake, walk in a northerly direction along the west side of the Cove. A line of magnificent plane trees is on the left,

and ahead is a wisteria arbor built of wood in a rustic style much favored in the 19th century. The gnarled vines of the wisteria climb and entwine themselves throughout the framework structure. At mid-April, this arbor, as well as a similar one just inside the West 72nd Street entrance, is massed with clusters of violet and purple blossoms.

A few paces further along the walk, a paved pathway on the right leads down to the edge of the Lake and to the West Drive Landing. This substantial wooden shelter is another of the four remaining passenger boat landings. It was reconstructed in 1970 in the original form but with heavier timber and without ornamental carving. A secluded spot surrounded by vegetation, the landing offers a splendid view of the west Lake, Bow Bridge, the Ramble shoreline, Hernshead and the Ladies Pavilion off to the left. It is also a good spot to feed the ducks, or even the swans when they deign to stop by.

Hernshead

Continuing northward along the Lake, a short stroll brings you to Hernshead Landing, also a former boat stop rebuilt as a shelter. It has a stunning view of the Lake. As you face the water, the promontory jut-

The Ladies Pavilion at Hernshead served as a shelter for horsecar passengers at the south entrance of the park until the early part of this century.

ting boldly into the Lake on the left is known as Hernshead. "Hern" is an archaic English pronunciation of heron, and from the landing the site's rocky outline does bear a resemblance to a heron's head. Herons as well as egrets are fairly common sights on the Lake, but the wading birds stay clear of Hernshead, where there may be too much activity these days for their comfort.

A good look around Hernshead should not be missed. In recent years, it has been nicely landscaped, and the area just inside the main entryways is lush with vegetation. In the spring, it bursts into color as bluebells, pink and blue ephemerals and multi-hued azaleas begin to bloom. Other plants along the pathway range from mayapple and barberry to snakeroot, ferns, and vivid fall-blooming asters. After a bit, the curving path takes you to a different, more picturesque part of Hernshead, which includes the Ladies Pavilion and the splendid rocks overlooking the Lake. You also can reach this part of the promontory, and bypass the plantings, by taking the stepping-stone path along its southern shoreline.

The Ladies Pavilion

This ornate structure has been called "a delectable Victorian fantasy in cast iron," and it is an apt description. It is replete with imaginative ironwork on railings, columns and arcades, and carries a jaunty row of finials on its roof. Designed by Mould in 1871, it originally served as a shelter for horsecar passengers waiting at the Eighth Avenue and 59th Street park

entrance. After about forty years, it was moved to make way for the construction of the Maine Monument in 1912-1913, and erected at the present site. There it suffered long periods of neglect, and in 1971 the dilapidated structure was knocked down by vandals.

Fortunately, the pieces of the Pavilion were salvaged and reassembled during a restoration in the early 1970s. This time, to thwart future vandalization, the building was anchored with steel rods sunk into a three-and-a-half-foot-deep concrete foundation. It was also fitted with a new metal-covered wooden roof with eaves supported by ornamental rafters. On several later occasions, damage done by lakeside weather and hoodlums required additional renovations, the latest ones being in the early 1980s, when masonry and roof repairs were made and stolen finials and small ironwork pieces were replaced. Today, although inconsistent maintenance sometimes leaves its dull grey and green paint worn down to the metal, the Pavilion is in excellent overall condition.

Before leaving Hernshead, make a point of exploring the massive outcropping of bedrock schist and granite at the end of the promontory. Geologists find much to study in this complex and fascinating rock mass. Other visitors, especially the agile, may wish to scramble around on it, inspecting its many rugged surfaces and climbing to the top. This cliff overlooking the water provides a wide-ranging view of the Lake and the surrounding shorelines.

Balcony Bridge

After returning to the pathway outside Hernshead, continue northward until you come to Balcony Bridge. Supporting the West Drive, this stone structure spans a small inlet connecting the Lake and what was originally the Ladies Pond. Once reserved for female ice-skaters, this westernmost finger of the Lake was filled in during the 1930s. The bridge itself gets its name from the two small, bench-lined balconies inset on its east side, both of which afford exceptional views of the Lake and the Manhattan skyline. Designed by Vaux, the bridge has handsome sandstone railings with an open quatrefoil pattern. For a good side view of the structure, with its multi-colored elliptical arch, visitors must look from the Ramble or from a rowboat on the Lake.

Bank Rock Bridge

A few paces further north will take you to Bank Rock Bridge. Though singularly lacking in charm, the span across a narrow arm of the Lake known as Bank Rock Bay is a major, heavily-used link to the woodsy Ramble. Both the bay and the bridge are named for the steep rocky banks that rise on the eastern shore.

Known as the Oak Bridge when it was built in 1860, it had an elegantly constructed balustrade and posts made of white oak fortified by thin cast-iron panels. The floorboards were of yellow pine. But the wooden bridge was expensive to maintain, and many years of halfhearted maintenance and unimaginative restoration took their toll. The present structure is built atop the original stone abutments and oak trestles, but the walkway now has a railing of spiked steel pipe and a floor of ordinary wooden planks.

By mid-summer the bay disappears under a thick layer of green algae but still manages to attract the occasional black-crowned Night Heron and myriad waterfowl in search of a meal.

The Ramble

An artfully contrived wilderness in the heart of the park, the Ramble is one of the more inspired creations of Olmsted and Vaux. Located just north of the Lake, it is a thickly wooded, thirty-six-acre tract marked by rugged outcrops, steep cliffs, a meandering stream called the Gill, and a tangle of pathways that lead to unexpected scenes and then disappear into the dense greenery. It is easy to get lost in the Ramble, as many tourists and even park regulars can attest.

On any given day, it is not unusual to find botanists, geologists, bird watchers, painters and just plain nature lovers along the paths or on the shoreline. They come out of scholarly curiosity, a craving for esthetic pleasure, or the simple need of the city dweller to take leave of the asphalt and breathe the revivifying air of this miniature woodland. For many years, gay males have also found the Ramble a congenial place to meet.

A Bird-Watchers Paradise

Though the Ramble is a visual treat throughout the daytime, park connoisseurs regard the morning hours as the choicest. In pleasant weather, the air is cool, the birds flutter, swoop and hop about in search of food—or maybe just for the fun of it. Few people are on the pathways: sometimes only Conservancy gardeners and binocular-toting bird watchers. The regular birders arrive in the Ramble in the early hours, often meeting at the Bank Rock Bridge or Loeb Boathouse for their daily sojourn in pursuit of avian lore.

It comes as a surprise to many people, including most New Yorkers, to hear that Central Park, and the Ramble especially, is a mecca for bird watchers. They would be even more surprised to learn that the publication *Birds of Central Park* listed 275 bird species as seen in the park in the year 1996. In fact, the Audubon Society has ranked the Ramble among the top fifteen bird-watching locales in the country, along with such prestigious sites as Yosemite and the Everglades.

How is this possible in the middle of Manhattan? Basically because the city is smack in the middle of major migratory flyways, and during the spring and fall migrations, when millions of birds take to the air, a green oasis like Central Park is an inviting spot to visit for food and rest. The forested, well-watered Ramble is the area most favored by the birds as a temporary stopover.

Creation of the Ramble

Back when the park was being built, Olmsted envisioned the Ramble as a romantic "wild garden." After the

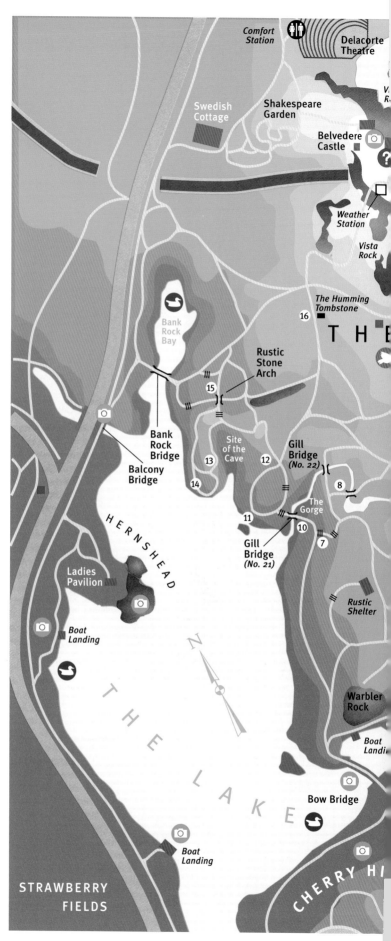

Comfort
Station

Delacorte
Theatre

Swedish
Cottage

Shakespeare
Garden

Belvedere
Castle

Weather
Station

Vista
Rock

The Humming
Tombstone

16

T H E

Bank
Rock Bay

Rustic
Stone
Arch

15

Bank
Rock
Bridge

Balcony
Bridge

Site
of the
Cave

13

12

Gill
Bridge
(No. 22)

8

14

The
Gorge

11

10

Gill
Bridge
(No. 21)

7

H E R N S H E A D

Ladies
Pavilion

Rustic
Shelter

Boat
Landing

N

Warbler
Rock

Boat
Landi

T H E   L A K E

Bow Bridge

Boat
Landing

STRAWBERRY
FIELDS

CHERRY HI

URTLE POND

Information — Information
Phone — Phone
Food Service — Food Service
Rest Rooms — Rest Rooms
Statue, Monument, Fountain — Statue, Monument, Fountain
Photo Site — Photo Site
Waterfowl Site — Waterfowl Site
Birding Site — Birding Site

Police Call Box ■

⑥ Numbers refer to text descriptions

ry Luce Nature
ervatory

Fire Command
Station

Comfort
Station

CEDAR
HILL

Iphigene's
Walk

Bonfire
Rock

AMBLE

PELO MEADOW

Source
of the
Gill

Still Hunt
Sculpture

Azalea
Pond
Bridge

Azalea
Pond   9

Balanced
Rock

Bicycle
Rental

Willow
Rock

5

2

1

Bamboo

3

Willow
Oven

Bamboo

LOEB
BOATHOUSE
CAFE

Rowboat
Rental

The Point   4

Trefoil
Arch

Bethesda
Terrace

Bethesda
Fountain

terrain was cleared of undesirable stone and plant life, and after its swampy wetlands were filled, a forest of richly varied trees, shrubs and flowers was planted. A stream was created and made to wind through the landscape, forming pools and splashing down rocky slopes before emptying into the Lake. Charming paths, rustic bridges, a mysterious cave, an ancient-looking stone arch and exotic birds like peacocks and guinea fowl provided additional fairy-tale touches.

The Ramble was one of the first sections of the park opened to the public, a few years before the start of the Civil War, and it was enormously popular from the start. Clarence Cook, the preeminent art critic of the time, noted that it was a purely man-made piece of landscape gardening but praised it highly. "Nature having done almost nothing, art had to do all," he wrote. "Yet the art of concealing art was hardly ever better illustrated."

The Decline of the Ramble

Over time, of course, Olmsted's luxuriant wild garden could not withstand the coming and going of millions of visitors each year. Budgetary constraints made the care and feeding of peacocks seem extravagant, and for many decades even ordinary maintenance was neglected in the Ramble. As a result, the carefully devised landscape evolved in a totally unplanned way into something more akin to real woodland. Ornamental birds were replaced by rabbits, frogs, turtles and raccoons, uninvited squatters who knew how to live off the land. Overgrown meadows, unpruned shrubs and dead trees proved highly desirable lodgings for small animals and a great number of birds.

Still, overuse and abuse continued to take a toll. In the 1950s a much-needed restoration brought fresh topsoil and new plantings to its unkempt and badly-treated sections. But the usual wear and tear ensued and in 1981 the newly-formed Conservancy launched a major effort to renew the beauty of the Ramble. The Point, a peninsula jutting into the Lake across from the Bethesda Terrace, was cleared of brush and dead wood, its worn surface was covered with fresh earth and replanted with hundreds of shrubs and trees, and its shoreline boulders were realigned to prevent erosion.

So far, so good. But then a number of trees in the Ramble were cut down to recover some of its original sunny glades and reclaim something dear to the park's founding fathers—a clear line of sight between Bethesda Terrace and the Belvedere Castle atop Vista Rock. The reaction from woods lovers, and especially the bird watchers, was explosive. Outraged letters poured in to the newspapers, the Linnaean and Audubon societies protested, and a petition denouncing "the mass destruction of mature and irreplaceable trees" was signed by 3000 people and presented to the Parks Department.

At a raucous public hearing, park spokesmen explained that only twenty trees had been culled, that new tree species were being added to the Ramble during the restoration, and that their actions were nothing more than "healthy land management." Critics said sixty trees were felled, and bird watchers claimed the bird population would be decimated if the restoration were not halted. "Hell hath few furies such as one of these," said a park official about the birders.

As a result of the bitterness, work on the Ramble came to a halt and restoration efforts were paralyzed for years. Not until 1990, when the antagonists were somewhat reconciled, was a slow, step-by-step program agreed upon. A series of careful, low-impact projects was initiated, an incremental restoration that is still in progress. The bird watchers, and others, seem pleased with the results. The birds continue to sing, unaware of the fracas over their welfare.

⊕ A Tour of the Ramble

To see the Ramble, allot yourself a few hours and put on a good pair of walking shoes. As mentioned above, it is easy to get lost, but the map (page 68) should guide you to its places of interest and to ways in and out of the area. Any of the daytime hours are excellent times to enjoy the scenery and wildlife, but the hours after nightfall are definitely not recommended. In general, Central Park is one of the safest parts of the city, and it is well-policed. But it is never advisable for anyone, casual visitor or park veteran, to take a solitary stroll in secluded, wooded areas like the Ramble after dark.

There are three main entryways

Ignaz Anton Pilat

Chief Landscape Gardener of the Park

"Ignaz A. Pilat is the gentleman to whom the public is indebted for the fine effects in the arrangement of plants." This comment in the *New York Evening Post* in 1866 about Pilat's role in the creation of Central Park was an immense understatement. As chief gardener of the massive project, the Austrian political refugee had led the hands-on job of converting a landscape scarred by the building effort into a model of botanical excellence.

Pilat came to the park with impressive credentials. He earned a degree at the University of Vienna, started his training in gardening at the university's famed botanical garden and later became its assistant director. He also wrote a well-regarded work on horticulture and landscaped homes in the American South before being hired in 1858 to supervise the gardening of the park.

Under Olmsted's overall guidance, Pilat was in charge of a band of German immigrants who dominated the gardening department. He directed them as they cleared and fertilized the earth, planted hundreds of thousands of trees, shrubs, herbs and vines, and created grassy meadows and lawns. At Pilat's order, they also rearranged boulders and shaped slopes, often clashing with engineers who had little concern for landscaping. It was well known that he was far more expert than anyone on botanical matters, and the gardeners on the job took orders only from "Mr. Pilat."

Like Olmsted and Vaux, Pilat was dedicated to the park. In addition to the gardening, he was in charge of two nurseries that propagated seed and nurtured plants from local suppliers. Pilat also acquired many uncommon species, which he tended with great skill. Under his management, the nurseries provided the park with almost 90,000 shrubs and trees, adding much to its botanical diversity.

Pilat, who died in 1870 at the age of 50, did not live to see the completion of Central Park. But he had made a unique contribution and it was well recognized by the park's designers. A few years earlier, Vaux had taken the liberty of sending Pilat a $500 gift on behalf of the Olmsted-Vaux partnership. "We are well aware that much has depended on you," Vaux wrote, "and that if our design has been virtually carried out, it is [due to] your persistent adhesion to its letter, and to its spirit."

to the Ramble on its Lake side: the path at the northwest end of the Loeb Boathouse; the Bow Bridge, in the center of the park at the level of 73rd Street; and the Bank Rock Bridge, near the West Drive at the level of 78th Street. Several other paths lead into the Ramble on the north, including two from the steps of the Belvedere Castle.

We begin our tour on the pathway between the Boathouse and the parking lot ❶ that leads past a massive, heavily-folded cliff face and up a steep incline. Take the first sharp left onto the path along the fence. About thirty paces past the end of the fence the path branches in three directions. Bear left onto the unpaved path leading south toward the Point ❷. This rocky, wooded promontory points like a dagger across the Lake at the Bethesda Terrace.

The Point

About sixty feet past a black iron railing, a clearing on the right ❸ opens to a rocky cliff overlooking a cove of the Lake known as the Willow Oven. The name comes from the willows overhanging the shoreline below and the cove's reputation for unusually high temperatures. The cliff provides a fine view of the Lake and the woodland across the cove, as well as a fascinating close-up of the birdlife in the upper canopies of its many trees.

Continuing southward, the narrow dirt and gravel path winds through dense patches of barberry, jetbead, shrub dogwood and thorny multiflora rose bushes. Normally the haunt of cardinals, blue jays and sparrows, during migration times these shrubs also attract more than twenty species of warbler. At the end of the Point ❹, the views of the Terrace directly ahead and of Bow Bridge to the west have long been tempting subjects for photographers.

Returning from the Point to the paved path, swing left around the shoreline of the cove, or Willow Oven, until you come to Willow Rock ❺. A flat outcrop of bedrock schist overlooking the cove from the west, it of course takes its name from the nearby willow trees. Like the Point, it is a prime bird-watching spot, since many species come to the cove below to forage in the secluded thicket of willow, ash and elderberry. Early morning visitors sometimes see resident groundhogs among the boulders along the Point or surprise a heron stalking the shoreline for food.

Further along the path, past thick, reedy growth and some open lakeside spaces, a large boulder ❻ near the water often catches the attention of strollers. Why? Not because of its intrinsic geological interest, but because a fissure in the tapered rock creates an image of a smiling dinosaur. To complete the picture, aspiring artists occasionally paint eyes and a nose on the stone, but their work is soon undone by the Conservancy's graffiti brigade.

Warbler Rock

On the opposite side of the path a large rock outcropping rises towards the north. This is Warbler Rock, another place favored by the birders, and it is an easy climb for a view of the surroundings if you are reasonably agile. For a brief side tour, find the paved walk at the back of the rock. Forty paces or so will take you to the Rustic Shelter, a large open-air structure of rough-hewn logs. Of fifteen such summerhouses built in the 19th century, it is the only one remaining—with help from a repair job in 1982—in its original form. Other summerhouses now in the park, including the Cop Cot in the lower park—have been totally rebuilt.

Returning to the lakeside, the path leads past one of four remaining 19th century boat landings.

This little wooden structure is a good place to rest, to watch the rowers go by and to admire the exquisite ironwork of Bow Bridge.

As the path turns to cross the bridge, instead take a sharp right and head north along the edge of the Lake's west lobe. Along the way, the shoreline provides good views of the Lake and the Hernshead (page 65) as well as the historic, multi-gabled Dakota apartment building, the twin-towered San Remo and other buildings rising above the tree line on Central Park West.

The Gill

At lamppost #7525, a stone stairway on the right ❼ marks the start of a side tour of the Gill, as the Ramble's sprightly little stream is officially known. (All park lampposts used to contain embossed locator numbers—near the top of the base, with the first two numbers indicating the nearest cross street; many still do, although it takes a bit of searching.) At the top of the stairs, take a left at the first intersection, then take a right across the rustic bridge over the stream ❽. Keeping the stream on your right, follow the path as it curves left and then right to another little bridge, the Azalea Pond Bridge.

Azalea Pond

The pond to the left ❾, a small body of water fed by the Gill and named for the century-old azalea plants on its southern edge, is probably the most active bird-watching spot in the park.

It is also the site of an unofficial feeding station maintained by the regular birders at their own expense during the cold times of the year, usually from October or November to the middle of April, when the food supply of insects, seeds and berries is non-existent or scarce. Then a visitor will see an array of peculiar-looking feeders hooked to branches of nearby cork trees by twisted wire coat hangers. The feeders are mainly seed-filled plastic soda bottles with small feeding holes cut in the sides, little sticks for perches and Frisbees to keep squirrels from getting to the food. These seeds, augmented by chunks of suet attached to tree trunks, and by bits of bread and lumps of dog food scattered on the frozen ground, help the wintering sparrows, jays, woodpeckers and chickadees make it through until springtime.

By closing off a fissure between two rock outcrops, Olmsted and Vaux created a cave that could be approached from the Lake by rowboat. While the entrance has since been sealed, the site and the original stone staircase carved into solid rock are still visible from a nearby path.

The Source of the Gill

Back across the bridge, the path along the pond's north rim leads up the stream to its starting point, a naturalistic grouping of boulders that is called the Source of the Gill. Actually, the water comes from the New York City reservoir and flows from a pipe deep inside the rocks. Although rumor has it that the flow is regulated by a faucet hidden nearby, the stream sometimes overflows its shallow banks because of snowmelt or heavy rainfall. But no matter. The Source is usually a pretty place, with trees and shrubs surrounding a narrow pool much favored by dog owners as a place for man's best friend to swim—especially during the dog-days of summer.

Keeping the Gill on your left, return to the pathway on the east side of the Lake. Follow it a few paces to the Gill Bridge ❿, another little rustic bridge that crosses the stream after passing through The Gorge and just before it flows into the Lake. Two rough-hewn benches give strollers a chance to rest and enjoy the sight and sound of the water splashing from a dam of massive boulders that underpins yet another bridge that spans the ravine a short distance upstream. After crossing the bridge and entering the western part of the Ramble, take the path to the left ⓫. After a short distance, a steep but accessible dirt path on the left opens onto another fine view of the Lake and to the seasonal gathering of waterfowl that bask on the nearby rock or the fallen branch that extends out into the water. Besides the always resident Mallards and Cormorants, one can occasionally get a close-up look at a Black-Crowned Night Heron or a brilliantly-colored Wood Duck.

Continuing on to the next intersection ⓬, take another left along the pipe rail. This scenic route takes you up a steep slope and around the edge of the overgrown, silt-choked cove below.

The Cave

As you walk, look down below the curving pipe rail and you will eventually see a flat ledge cluttered with rocks and debris. Leaning over the rail ⓭, you will be able to make out the entrance, among the large boulders, to what once was the Cave. This was a fanciful creation of Olmsted and Vaux, who had a natural cleft in the bedrock roofed over with giant boulders and made into a dark, eerie cavern. For many years, it was a popular spot for adventuresome parkgoers, especially rowers who could approach the Cave from the waters of the cove below.

Perched upon Vista Rock, Belvedere Castle looks down at a newly restored Turtle Pond. The castle houses the Henry Luce Nature Observatory.

The Cave was closed in the 1920s because it had become the haunt of tramps, as they were then called, and was considered dangerous. A stairway, chiseled out of solid rock, and still in evidence, leads down to the entrance now sealed off with stone and cement.

Now follow the pipe rail to its end, and take a sharp left down a small pathway to the Lake's edge. This is one of the best places of all to view the skyline of Central Park West and Central Park South **14**.

Rustic Stone Arch

Continue on the path, up the hill until you come to an intersection. A left turn will take you to the Rustic Stone Arch **15**, a rough but finely wrought structure that was designed to add a touch of romantic antiquity to this area of the Ramble.

From the top of the arch, you will see that it spans a rocky gorge, the south wall a natural outcropping, the north wall man-made of huge boulders. For a closer view, cross the bridge, circle around to the right and go down the steps to the footpath that leads under the high, arched structure. You will note that its stones, all pieces of bedrock schist, are shaped and fitted so precisely that gravity and friction, not cement, are holding the arch together. The setting makes some visitors think of faraway places and long gone times.

Return above to the path heading northward and toward the upper reaches of the Ramble. After a bit, the terrain becomes less thickly wooded and you come upon an intersection with a grass clearing on the right. Standing at the edge of it is a large rectangular stone block referred to by bird-watching regulars as the Humming Tombstone **16**. A well-known rendezvous for the birders who meet there in hopes of spotting an unusual nesting in the thicket adjoining nearby Tupelo Meadow, it is also the mechanism that turns the lampposts in the area on and off.

Tupelo Meadow

Continuing eastward past the southern approaches of Vista Rock and Belvedere Castle on the left brings you to Tupelo Meadow on the right.

One of the few open green spaces in the Ramble, the meadow also has some of its handsomest trees. One of them is a prominently situated sour gum tree, a graceful variety of tupelo with brilliant fall color. It is regarded by some as the loveliest tree in Central Park.

Continuing on, the path winds past a large outcropping known as Bonfire Rock. A nearby path, Iphigene's Walk, commemorates Iphigene Ochs Sulzberger, president of the Central Park Association from 1934 to 1950 and a leading preservationist in the fight to maintain the park in Olmsted and Vaux's original vision. Using her family's highly influential newspaper, *The New York Times,* she denounced any plan that threatened to offer the park up to commercial interests or deprive the public of places where they might peaceably commune with nature.

Belvedere Castle

Standing atop the rocky summit of Vista Rock just north of the 79th Street transverse, the Belvedere Castle is the most picturesque architectural feature in the park. A rugged stone structure with a peaked tower, it was designed by

Calvert Vaux in a typically Victorian mixture of styles, including Norman, Gothic and even a touch of Moorish. For a superb view of the castle, walk along the northern rim of the Turtle Pond. From that vantage, its entire length rises dramatically from the dark, ancient cliff like a medieval fortress.

But Belvedere Castle is not only to be admired from a distance. Its three ascending terraces offer visitors commanding views of the landscape and wonderful photo opportunities. They are favorite haunts of the park's bird watchers, and particularly the hawk watchers, a band of enthusiasts who track the activities of the magnificent raptors. The castle also serves as an information center, a home to the Henry Luce Nature Observatory, and a data-gathering outpost for the United States Weather Bureau.

Vista Rock

Whether approaching the castle from the southern edge of the Turtle Pond, or through the Shakespeare Garden, or via the narrow paths leading from the Ramble, visitors will be climbing up the slopes of Vista Rock. A massive outcropping of schist created hundreds of mil-

lions of years ago, it was seen by Olmsted and Vaux as the perfect site for a romantic castle that would serve as a focal point in the park's landscape.

Even before entering the castle, visitors are drawn immediately to the large wooden loggia and the curved parapet wall facing northward over the park. Down below, beyond the sheer drop of the rock face, the scenery ranges from the Delacorte Theater and Turtle Pond in the foreground to the more distant Great Lawn and the Fifth Avenue skyline.

History of the Castle

The lower terrace is also a good place to examine the construction of the castle and ponder its history. Designed by Vaux in 1867 and completed in 1872, the Belvedere was for many years an enormously popular destination for parkgoers. But in 1919, it was closed to the general public when it was occupied by the U.S. Weather Bureau.

To accommodate offices and instruments, many alterations were made, including the removal of the tower's peak to make a flat roof space for monitoring equipment. In the early 1960s, the bureau installed an automatic weather recording system, most of which is enclosed behind a rectangle of Cyclone fencing to the south of the castle, and removed the entire staff to other locations.

Neglect and vandalism soon brought the vacant Belvedere to a sorry state. Park-lovers complained loudly, and in the early 1980s improved city finances and private foundation money generated by the newly formed Conservancy made it possible to carry out a major restoration. The damaged and graffiti-marked parapets were repaired, missing pieces of masonry were replaced, the interior was renovated, and the peaked tower was returned to its original condition. Reopened to the public in 1982, it housed a Learning Center that conducted educational and cultural programs until 1996, when it was replaced by the Nature Observatory.

Henry Luce Nature Observatory
Entering the castle from the lower terrace, visitors find an information center staffed by helpful park volunteers. An adjoining room holds a major part of the Nature Observatory. Though its walls and floor are of dark stone, this is a light and airy space full of telescopes, microscopes, turtle and fish tanks, fossil replicas, plant specimens, and of course desks and benches. Here school groups or interested visitors can learn some of the skills for observing nature, with a particular emphasis on the park's great range of plants and animals.

A narrow stone stairway enclosed in the tower winds up to a chamber on the second level. Another section of the Nature Observatory, it has additional child-sized desks, information about birds and bird watching, and a box that produces bird calls at the push of a button. On one wall is a video display of the current weather conditions in the park. This report, which includes temperature, wind velocity, precipitation and visibility, is updated every minute by the U.S. Weather Bureau located in Brookhaven, L.I. The bureau gets its data from the instruments in the fenced area south of the castle and others located on the top of the tower.

Through an arched doorway is the first of the roof terraces. Graced by small corner overlooks called *bartizans*, its loftier elevation affords a somewhat more extensive view than the level below. But an even more striking one awaits further up the tower stairway. On this topmost terrace, the castle rewards visitors with a superb panoramic scene, encompassing a large part of the surrounding park landscape and the skyline in all directions. Not surprisingly, a frequent sound heard here is the click of cameras.

This spot also is one of the prime favorites of the hawk groupies, especially on crisp mornings from September to December when the annual southward migration is under way. Most carry powerful binoculars and talk knowledgeably about sharp-shinned or broad-tailed hawks, not to mention kestrels, ospreys and falcons, all of which are seen in the park. When one of the birders cries out "Hawk up!" and gives a location, up go all the binoculars and a quiet chatter begins: "I see it, I think it's a shinnie." "No, it's too dark, it's a broadtail." And so forth. After a while, they stand around and confer on what they had seen, at times even sharing bits of arcane hawk lore with inquisitive visitors.

Before descending to leave the castle, it is hard to resist a final visit to the parapet for a good look at the scene spread out below. It is magnificent and rightfully deserves the name it was given: Belvedere—a beautiful view.

Turtle Pond
An elegant little body of water below the cliffs of Belvedere Castle, the Turtle Pond is not only a scenic delight but a wildlife habitat of considerable interest. It is, of course, home to many turtles, but its waters and thickly planted shorelines also shelter a variety of fish and frogs. Waterfowl are common sights, and the pond has been celebrated for the abundance of its darting, hovering dragonflies. During the quieter morning hours, cormorants and giant blue herons often come hunting for food.

Like the Great Lawn to the north, the Turtle Pond occupies part of the huge empty pit created when the obsolete old Croton Reservoir was drained in 1930. In 1934 Parks Commissioner Moses had the lower part of the space made into a modest pond he grandly called Belvedere Lake. It was later renamed the Turtle Pond by Commissioner Stern.

During a major restoration car-

Above: In the Shakespeare Garden, a sundial set among seasonal plantings. Inset: Red poppies provide a bright color accent in spring.

ried out from 1995 to 1997, the Turtle Pond was cleared of large amounts of silt, its boundaries were enlarged and freshly landscaped, and a wildlife island was created.

Before restoration, the pond's turtle population was chiefly composed of snapping turtles and red-eared sliders, although a few musk turtles, painted turtles and cooters were among them. Fish included bass, perch, bluegill, pumpkinseed, brown bullhead, golden shiner and goldfish. But during restoration, the pond was drained and its occupants were "temporarily relocated." Since renovation, the Conservancy reports, some turtles and fish have found their way back into the pond, but it will not be officially stocked until the new habitat has further evolved.

A walk around the pond offers an assortment of small pleasures. Near its west end a wooden pier leads out over the water and offers superb views of Belvedere Castle, the island and the entire shoreline. The grassy area on the pond's north side is ornamented with boulders to sit on and the water's edge is richly stocked with varieties of aquatic plant life that attract insects, birds and turtles. Designated as a quiet zone (loud music and noisy activities are barred), this bucolic setting is a good site to read, meditate or simply enjoy the surrounding beauty.

Shakespeare Garden

On a steep rocky hillside, tucked between the Belvedere Castle and the Swedish Cottage, the Shakespeare Garden is not the easiest place to find. But it is an enchanting hideaway and well worth searching out. Henry J. Stern, Parks Commissioner under mayors Edward Koch and Rudolph Giuliani, has aptly called it "a little treasure in Central Park which most people won't know about."

William Shakespeare was, among other things, quite a plant-lover. In his plays and poems, he included the names of 200 trees, shrubs, wildflowers and herbs. The park's four-acre Shakespeare Garden, totally redesigned in the 1980s in an informal, "romantic" style, now has about half of them. Notable among them is a large Mulberry tree, whose branches overspread the rustic entryway alongside the Swedish Cottage. By some accounts, the handsome tree has grown from a cutting taken in Shakespeare's mother's garden in Stratford-on-Avon.

At first glance, the garden appears to be something of a jumble. Roses are scattered helter-skelter. Lilies sprout from patches of fern. Only about ten of the thickly planted flowers and herbs have bronze plaques nearby with appropriate quotes from the plays. But there is much art behind the apparent lack of order. The wonderful variety of plants are grouped by colors, textures and bloom time, and stone pathways with wooden benches wind in and out among them, leading the visitor from one visual delight to another. Unless she is busy planting, weeding, or directing her crew, the knowledgeable gardener will identify plants for the curious.

Many of the flora have names with a distinctly Elizabethan ring: wormwood and quince, lark's heel and rue, eglantine and columbine, primrose, flax and cowslip. Opium poppies and poisonous hemlock, both of which were mentioned frequently by Shakespeare but not deemed appropriate for a public park, were replaced by less potent varieties.

In the early days of the park, the garden did not exist. The rocky slope to the west of Belvedere Castle was merely a woodsy extension of the Ramble. Not until 1913 was it transformed into a Victorian style rock garden called the Garden of the Heart. In 1916, the tricentennial of Shakespeare's death, that was turned into a garden dedicated to his memory and filled with plants mentioned in his works. A marble bust of

Bold white peonies blooming under the partial shade of yews delight visitors to the garden in late spring.

the great poet and dramatist was placed on the site.

The following decades were not kind to the garden. The Shakespeare Society of New York, the major force behind its creation and maintenance, disbanded in 1929. One city administration after another treated it as an unwanted stepchild. From neglect, the garden became a jungle of weeds; the bust apparently was destroyed by vandals.

In 1975, when conditions in the garden were at their worst, a group of dedicated volunteers called the Shakespeare Gardeners came to the rescue. For eleven years, they nurtured the surviving plants and introduced many new ones. Then in 1986, after the Samuel and May Rudin Foundation donated funds for the garden, a major restoration was begun. Totally replanted and redesigned by landscape architects to achieve an "unkempt, wild flavor," its granite walls were replaced by wooden fences, its asphalt hexagonal block paths with gray flagstone. The garden also was expanded to include an upper portion of the slope, uniting it visually with the imposing Belvedere Castle.

The quiet paths of the Shakespeare Garden are a special attraction. Here, clusters of brilliant red tulips bloom near a spreading crab apple tree.

Judging by public response and critical judgments, the restored

Shakespeare Garden has been a great success since its opening in 1989. Beautifully tended and highly picturesque, it is hardly suprising that it is a favorite spot for painters and garden-lovers. Bird watchers come to see cardinals and cedar waxwings build nests in the spring, or to spy on the saw-whet owls that roost in the evergreen bushes in winter. Actors in the plays at the nearby Delacorte Theater occasionally drop by. Can they be coming to commune with the spirit of you-know-who?

For the most part, those who come to the garden are ordinary folks, school groups, people who have lost their way, and tourists. Some repeat aloud the words on the plaques, a favorite being the well-known lines of the sprite Ariel in *The Tempest*: "Where the bee sucks, there suck I; In a cowslip's bell I lie." Nearby, bees are indeed sipping nectar at a rose bush. But a few visitors seem determined to ask the gardener: "What about cowslip? Do you really have it here?" At that, she usually bends down, sorts through a mixed flower bed and touches a perky, little yellow blossom. "Cowslip," she says with a slightly triumphant smile.

Swedish Cottage

Whether the show is "Goldilocks and the Three Bears," "Gulliver," or "Rumpelstiltskin," children and parents with children love the Swedish Cottage Marionette Theatre. Located on the park's west side at the level of 79th Street, the building itself is a charming replica of a 19th century Swedish country schoolhouse. The marionettes are made by the same hidden hands that pull their strings and bring them to life on the little stage. This is a fairy-tale place, where the laughter of children is heard throughout the year.

The cottage was built in Sweden, primarily of Baltic fir, then shipped in sections to Philadelphia for display at the 1876 Centennial Exposition. In the following year, at Olmsted's urging, the building was purchased for $1,500 and reassembled at its present location in Central Park. During the decades that followed, it was used and misused for storage and for public bathrooms, as an entomological laboratory and as a Civil Defense District Headquarters during World War II. In 1947, it was turned over to the Parks Department's Traveling Marionette Theatre as a headquarters and workshop, and in 1973 a permanent theater was installed.

Performances at the cottage were halted in 1997, when it was closed for restoration after 120 years of continuous use. The natural wood exterior was cleaned and mended. Holes made by squirrels, mice and birds were repaired. Inside, the theater was given fresh pine paneling, a new stage decorated with Swedish motifs, a handsome midnight blue carpet and rows of shiny wooden benches for the audience. With brand-new lighting, heating and cooling systems, the old cottage was technologically contemporary when it reopened in May of 1998. Performances of classic children's stories are year-round and modestly priced. A cheerful room has been set aside for birthday parties or other private gatherings. For information, call (212) 988-9093.

Delacorte Theatre

The place to be on a fine summer's night is the Delacorte Theater. Located in mid-park on the western shore of the Turtle Pond, it is the home of the Shakespeare in the Park festival. For more than three decades the plays of the great dramatist have been presented each year from June through August. These free performances, often headed by stage or film stars such as Kevin Kline, Denzel Washington, Tracy Ullman and Patrick Stewart, have drawn enthusiastic crowds. New Yorkers and tourists often line up for hours or even overnight to get tickets on a first-come, first-served basis.

Built in 1960, the theater was financed in part by George Delacorte, the publisher and philanthropist, and in part by New York City. A large fan-shaped structure with rising tiers of seats and towering steel light fixtures, the Delacorte's low-lying exterior is plain and functional. But its front lawn area is nicely ornamented by two bronze statues of Shakespearean characters by Milton Hebald: a lyrical, stylized Romeo and Juliet; and a craggy depiction of the wizard Prospero and his daughter Miranda from *The Tempest*.

The festival itself was founded and originally directed by Joseph Papp, a feisty impresario who also started New York's non-profit Public Theater. Papp insisted that no admission be charged for the park

performances, but the Parks Department argued that maintenance costs would have to be covered by the festival, an arrangement which would have required an admission charge.

For weeks, the battle raged in the media. But in the end, public opinion sided with Papp and the Parks Department was forced to back down. Free Shakespeare has been one of the park's greatest cultural attractions ever since.

Tickets, two to a person, are available starting at 1 p.m. the day of the performance at the Delacorte or at the Public Theater, 425 Lafayette Street, near Astor Place. For information, call (212) 539-8655.

The Great Lawn

At first glance, the area known as the Great Lawn seems to be misnamed. The thirteen-acre oval in mid-park between 81st and 85th streets appears in fact to be a collection of extremely fine ball fields. But the expanse of emerald green grass between the diamonds can also be used by walkers, sunbathers and picnickers, and musical events are occasionally held there at night during the summer.

The larger Great Lawn "area" encompasses forty-one acres, including the Turtle Pond, the Arthur Ross Pinetum and some beautifully landscaped stretches to the east and west of the oval. All of these were part of an ambitious restoration project carried out from 1995 to 1996, and as a result all look quite wonderful. The Great Lawn itself, the space within the oval that once was much abused, is resplendent with lush bluegrass and eight carefully tended softball fields. As many as ten million people tread on the oval each year, and thousands of ball games are played each summer. To protect the revitalized lawn, strict rules have been imposed: no dogs, no ball games without a permit, no bikes, no frisbee throwing by more than two people, no soccer playing, except by children not wearing cleats.

The plant life that surrounds the oval, always impressive, is more vibrant than ever. The cherry trees on its perimeter flower gloriously from late March through April. Lining the pathways bordering the oval and in the terrain to its immediate east and west are a stunning variety of trees and shrubs, over 2000 of them planted during the restoration.

Like the neighboring Turtle Pond, the Great Lawn was created on space made available by the draining of the Croton Reservoir. Starting in 1934, an army of laborers, many paid by Depression Era federal relief programs, filled in the dried bed with thousands of truckloads of soil, planted the grass, trees and shrubs, and paved the peripheral pathways. Two years later, the Great Lawn was opened to the public.

The delight of many park devotees turned to dismay in the 1950s, when park officials bowed to public pressure and added ball fields with permanent backstops to the lawn. In the years that followed, special events that generated huge crowds were held there. In 1982 three-quarters of a million people crowded the Great Lawn to denounce the nuclear arms race. A Paul Simon concert in 1991 drew 600,000 to the oval, and a 1995 Mass conducted by Pope John Paul II attracted 350,000.

The city skyline provides a dramatic backdrop for this sweeping panoramic view of the lush expanse of green of the Great Lawn and one of six softball fields.

Not surprisingly, the punishment inflicted over the years by millions of feet and countless ball games finally reduced the greensward to an appalling condition. After the papal Mass, inspectors found that half the grass was dead, the ground was rock-hard and much of the topsoil had been eroded. "The Great Lawn," said Commissioner Stern, "is a dustbowl."

But not for long. In October 1995, the Conservancy and the Parks Department kicked off what they called the greatest restoration project in the history of Central Park. The lawn was blocked off to the public and the entire oval was dug up. An elaborate new system of drainage pipes was installed, and layers of soil mixtures designed to enhance drainage and rooting were laid. 500,000 square feet of Kentucky bluegrass were planted.

Unlike the past, a strict program of maintenance was also provided. Irrigation is now supplied by 270 computer-controlled sprinklers that pop up at the touch of a button. Mowing is done by vehicles with bulging wheels that are specially designed to prevent damage to the grass and topsoil. Overseeing the care of the entire area is the Keeper of the Great Lawn, an on-scene commander of five full-time employees plus seasonal workers and volunteers. In addition to many hands-on chores and the task of educating the public on acceptable park behavior, the Keeper also makes certain that the crowds at the annual summer appearances by the Metropolitan Opera and New York Philharmonic cause minimal damage to the lawn.

A four-foot-high wire fence encircles the oval and stands as a reminder that a strict new regime has come to the Great Lawn. The six gates are opened at 11 a.m.—on days when the Keeper thinks the lawn is in good enough condition for public use.

Summit Rock

Overlooking Central Park West at 83rd Street, Summit Rock is the highest point in the park at 137.5 feet. It is also a nicely landscaped, infrequently used retreat that has contributed some interesting if minor sidelights to New York legend and history.

The route most taken to the summit starts just above the Diana Ross Playground, then follows a path with rustic railings up a gently sloping hillside to an impressive stairway carved in the bedrock. This leads directly to the top. It is a beautiful spot, with an attractive mix of trees and shrubs, a flagstone terrace overlooking the park and a proximity to the apartment buildings to the west that somehow heightens the sense of elevation.

Legend has it that groups of local Indians used to gather here in pre-colonial days to discuss tribal affairs. In the early 19th century, the predominately African-American community of Seneca Village, uprooted later in the building of the park, adjoined Summit Rock to the northeast. European immigrants, largely Irish, lived in shanties on its slopes as well as in Seneca Village itself.

In 1921, an equestrian statue of Simón Bolívar, the man who led

many South American countries in their fight for independence from Spain, was placed atop Summit Rock. The Bolivar Hotel, now the Bolivar Apartments, still stands across the way on Central Park West. The bronze by Sally Jane Farnham was moved in 1951 to Central Park South and Sixth Avenue, where it now stands in Bolivar Plaza.

From time to time, Summit Rock—perhaps because it is the place in the park closest to heaven—has attracted groups with visionary ideas. In August of 1987, roughly 2000 people bearing candles gathered there before dawn one morning. For hours they rang bells, blew on conch shells and called out for universal peace and harmony. Onlookers said the demonstrators seemed visibly uplifted by their experience on Summit Rock. "We were guided to this place," said one of the leaders. "It is a spot of very high energy." Then they disappeared silently into Manhattan's West Side.

The Obelisk

Far from its original home at Heliopolis on the Nile River, the ancient Egyptian obelisk called "Cleopatra's Needle" is the park's most fascinating curiosity.

Standing on a landscaped knoll behind the Metropolitan Museum of Art, the stone stele inscribed with hieroglyphs was created roughly 3500 years ago by artisans and laborers toiling for the Pharaoh Thutmosis III. It is the largest outdoor antiquity in the city and by far the oldest man-made object in the park.

The obelisk's present site is a quiet green oasis screened from the busy East Drive by flowering trees and shrubbery. Measuring just over sixty-nine feet from base to tip, the granite monolith rises from its original pedestal and triple-tiered foundation. Its four corners are supported by ornamental bronze crabs. Visitors also will find plaques at the foot of the monument giving a brief history of the obelisk and a translation of the hieroglyphs—fulsome tributes to Thutmosis III and also to Ramses II, a later pharaoh who had paeans to his greatness chiseled onto the edges of the stone.

How is it that a relic of such a faraway and long-dead civilization is now standing in the middle of Central Park? Who brought it here and why?

Ancient Egypt was, in a sense, rediscovered in the 19th century. The occupation of the land by Napoleon's army in the early 1800s stirred tremendous interest in Egyptology among European and American archeologists, artists and travelers. Many visited Egypt and admired two obelisks located near the waterfront in Alexandria.

The pair, originally carved for Thutmosis III, had been erected with great ceremony before the Temple of the Sun in the sacred city of On (called Heliopolis by the Greeks) in 1443 B.C. Persian armies

Far left: One of the best known monuments in the park, the Obelisk, often called Cleopatra's Needle, is seen here in an 1878 photograph showing its former location in Alexandria, Egypt.

Near right: In its present site on Greywacke Knoll just behind The Metropolitan Museum of Art. One of a pair of obelisks originally built for the pharaoh Thutmosis III over 3500 years ago, it is the oldest man-made object in the park, rising 69 feet from the base to the top and weighing 220 tons.

Above: One of the reproductions of bronze crab supports dating from the time of the Roman occupation of Egypt.

razed the city in 525 B.C., toppling and partially scorching the obelisks. But they survived, and around 12 B.C. another conqueror, Rome's Augustus Caesar, had them shipped down the Nile to Alexandria. By then, the lower corners of the stones had been broken off, so the Romans had bronze supports in the form of sea crabs placed under them. (Two of the original crabs are in the Metropolitan Museum of Art; the other two were stolen in Egypt.)

The Romans also may have been the first to call the two obelisks *Cleopatra's Needles*, even though the Egyptian queen died twenty years before they arrived in Alexandria. There they stood long after the Romans departed, undisturbed until an earthquake struck the city in 1301, toppling but not breaking one of them. The obelisks remained in that condition until the 19th century, when the new interest in things Egyptian created an appetite for mementos of the pharaonic past. In 1831 the French removed an obelisk from the temple at Luxor and raised it in Paris. In 1877 the English were given the toppled Alexandria obelisk and took it off to London. Americans were now determined to bring the remaining obelisk to the United States.

A group of Americans, including Henry Hurlburt, the influential editor of the *New York World*, got railroad magnate William H. Vanderbilt to finance the project. Soon the U.S. State Department made known to the Khedive of Egypt, Ismail Pasha, its interest in acquiring the monument for America. Eager to cultivate ties with the United States, he readily agreed.

To execute the complicated task of removing, transporting and erecting the 220-ton stone, Hurlburt and Vanderbilt chose a U.S. Navy engineer, Lieutenant-Commander Henry Honeychurch Gorringe.

Gorringe, an ingenious and determined man, set to work. The foundation and pedestal of the obelisk had sunk well below the surface and had to be excavated. After conspicuously displaying the American flag on the obelisk to proclaim its new ownership, Gorringe had "one hun-

On January 22,1881, as reported in Harper's Weekly, at Gorringe's signal the obelisk moved "as easily as if it were the minute hand of a lady's watch....Two hundred and nineteen and a quarter tons of stone, distributed in a length of sixty-nine feet two inches, are not turned in mid-air every day."

dred Arabs, varying from ten to seventy years of age" clear away earth from around its base. It was then encased in protective wooden planking for the long journey. The bronze crabs were removed so that cables could tilt the stone and a steel tower with a turning mechanism designed by Gorringe could move it aloft into a horizontal position. It was then lowered slowly into a specially constructed wooden container on the ground, eased into the water and towed to Alexandria's port for shipment aboard the *Dessoug*, an English-built steamer purchased for the journey.

Gorringe also decided to take the pedestal and foundation stones to New York rather than constructing new ones on the final resting site. There was a reason for this: When the pedestal was moved from the foundation, beneath it was found a curious arrangement of marked stones and a trowel that some saw as proof of the ancient origins of Freemasonry. This secret order, then powerful in Europe and the United States, included Gorringe, Hulbert and Vanderbilt among its many members. As a result, it was decided to reposition the obelisk, pedestal and foundation in Central Park just as they had been arranged in Egypt.

On June 12, 1880, the *Dessoug* steamed out of port with its unique cargo. Having finally overcome many bureaucratic and engineering

obstacles, Gorringe had rolled the obelisk on cannonballs through the streets of Alexandria and into its hold through a temporary opening made in the side of the ship. At sea, the steamer sailed through several violent storms, had to have a crankshaft mended in the mid-Atlantic, but eventually reached Staten Island in New York Bay on July 20th.

The arrival of the obelisk created a sensation in New York. The city's newspapers were full of stories about the "mysterious" obelisk, including one that claimed its carvings told of Egypt's founding by ancient Mexicans. Everyone wanted to glimpse Cleopatra's Needle. "The report that the obelisk was to be disembarked," wrote Gorringe, "brought down to Staten Island a crowd of spectators, who occupied every spot from which a view of the work could be obtained."

After being rolled out of the hold, the obelisk was placed on pontoons and towed to Manhattan at the foot of 96th Street and the Hudson River. The final leg of its long journey to Central Park had begun. It was to be a laborious process.

The obelisk, still in its casing, was placed on a wooden framework, on the front of which was a powerful pile-driver engine attached to a winding drum. The framework, set on metal rollers, rested on wooden tracks. At every point of the way, an anchor chain borrowed from the

Dessoug connected the drum to a block fixed firmly in the street ahead. The engine pulled itself and the monolith forward by turning the drum and winding the chain around it.

As the obelisk inched across Manhattan's West Side, turning corners on a pivoting apparatus designed by Gorringe, crowds gathered to watch its progress. After crossing the park on the 86th Street Transverse, it turned down Fifth Avenue, then re-entered the park at 82nd Street and moved onto a high trestle for the final stretch. Sightseers, including men in stovepipe hats and women in bonnets, watched in bitter winter weather as it crept past the south end of the new Metropolitan Museum of Art. Not until January 5, 1881, one hundred and twelve days after landing in Manhattan, did Cleopatra's Needle reach the little hill it would stand on.

By this time, the foundation stones and the pedestal had been hauled to the site and installed. Members of the Masons had laid the foundation. The stones were placed exactly as they were in Alexandria and to the same points of the compass. As a kind of time capsule, a number of lead boxes of varying shapes were fit into spaces enclosed by the foundation steps. In the boxes were placed an odd assortment of items, including a facsimile of the Declaration of Independence, Freemason emblems, some hardware, a guide to Egypt, the Bible, Webster's dictionary and the works of Shakespeare.

On January 15, the obelisk was transferred from the trestle to Gorringe's turning structure, the same one used to remove it from its place in

Alexandria. The weighty stone was held for days in a horizontal position directly above the pedestal. On January 22, the date set for the raising, thousands of spectators congregated near the site. At a signal from Gorringe, the obelisk began to turn. It was halted briefly for a photograph at an angle of forty-five degrees and then turned again until it stood upright on the pedestal. The crowd cheered lustily and the Marine Band played rousing patriotic airs. Though the wooden casing and the turning machinery were yet to be removed, it was clear to everyone there that the long journey of Cleopatra's Needle was finally over.

Group of Bears

An exceptional piece of playground art, the *Group of Bears* by Paul Manship has won much favor with children, parents and photographers. The work stands in the pleasant Pat Hoffman Memorial Playground just south of the Metropolitan Museum of Art. There its three large brown bears face the entrance and command the attention of those who go in and many who pass by. Manship, a sculptor whose smooth, stylized art graces several sites in the park and many others around the city, first cast the grouping in 1932; this is a more recent casting.

Manship's Group of Bears *is magnetically attractive to children, whose affectionate stroking has shined their snouts and ears to a high polish since this bronze cast was erected in 1991.*

NORTH CENTRAL QUADRANT

84th Street North to the 97th Street Transverse

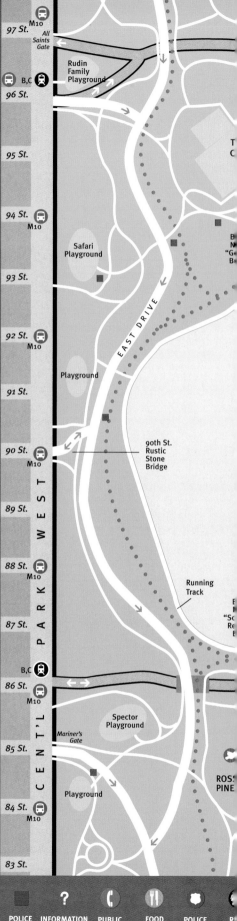

97 St. M10
All Saints Gate

96 St. B,C

Rudin Family Playground

95 St.

94 St. M10

Safari Playground

93 St.

92 St. M10

Playground

91 St.

90 St. M10

90th St. Rustic Stone Bridge

89 St.

88 St. M10

87 St.

B,C

86 St. M10

Spector Playground

Mariner's Gate

85 St.

84 St. M10

83 St.

EAST DRIVE

Running Track

ROSS PINE

PARK WEST

CENT'L

TRANSVERSES   ROADWAYS

● ● ● ● ● ●
BRIDLE PATHS

POLICE CALL BOX

? INFORMATION DESK

📞 PUBLIC PHONE

🍴 FOOD SERVICE

🛡 POLICE STATION

North Meadow
Recreation Center

97TH ST. TRANSVERSE

97 St.

Albert
Bertel
Thorvaldsen

Woodmen's
Gate

96 St.

M1,2,3,4

SOUTH
MEADOW

Oldest Tree
in the Park

Playground

95 St.

Running
Track

Int'l Center
of
Photography

94 St.

M1,2,3,4

North Gate
House

93 St.

SCALE
One city block
(north to south)
equals approximately
1/20th of a mile or
1/13th of a kilometer

The
Jewish
Museum

92 St.

M1,2,3,4

Rhododendron Mile
(87 St. to 95 St.)

Walking Tour
page 90

William
Thomas
Stead

91 St.

THE
RESERVOIR

Cooper
Hewitt
Museum

John
Purroy
Mitchel

90 St.

Engineer's
Gate

National
Academy
of Design

M1,2,3,4

89 St.

N

Solomon R.
Guggenheim
Museum

88 St.

F
I
F
T
H

W
E
S
T

D
R
I
V
E

87 St.

Running
Track

A
V
E
N
U
E

86 St.

M1,2,3,4

Bridge
No. 24
"Reservoir
Bridge
Southwest"

85TH ST. TRANSVERSE

South
Gate House

85 St.

CENTRAL PARK
PRECINCT

Volleyball
and
Basketball
Courts

Ancient
Playground

84 St.

M1,2,3,4

ROSS
PINETUM

GREAT
LAWN

MAP CONTINUED ON PAGE 52

METROPOLITAN
MUSEUM
OF ART

83 St.

ES M	MEN'S ROOM	MEDICAL ASSISTANCE	PHOTO SITE	STATUE, MONUMENT	WATERFOWL SITE	BIRDING SITE	SUBWAY STATION	BUS STOP

Ross Pinetum

Pines of many colors, sizes and shapes, pines from American forests and distant mountain slopes, all can be found flourishing at the Arthur Ross Pinetum (pronounced pine-ee-tum). This circular four-acre tract on the northwest corner of the Great Lawn boasts impressive elms and oaks as well, but the coniferous evergreen trees and shrubs are definitely the star attraction.

Counting everything from statuesque pine trees to squat, curiously-shaped pine shrubbery, the Pinetum includes hundreds of specimens from twenty different species. Among them are Black Pine from the Austrian Alpine regions, Stone Pine from Switzerland, Scotch Pine and Lacebark Pine, named for its oddly patterned bark. By far the most prevalent are White Pine, a sprightly native American variety, and Himalayan Pine, a type accustomed to clear mountain air yet thriving impressively in the park environment.

Not all pines have fared so well in the park over the years. For instance, the many conifers Olmsted planted on the west side of the park from 77th to 100th streets to create a scenic Winter Drive for carriages and sleighs were decimated by 20th century neglect and pollution. Now park horticulturalists plant hardier, more pollution-resistant pine varieties and give them plenty of attention.

The Pinetum was planted in 1971 with a donation from Arthur Ross, a long-time park benefactor. A playground area, designed during the Great Lawn restoration of 1995-1998, has a few swings but is less a playground than an extremely pleasant spot to picnic and enjoy the pines. Popular with young families, brown-bag lunchers and group picnickers, it is also an agreeable place for park visitors to stop and relax in a unique ambience.

The Reservoir

The Central Park Reservoir—officially the Jaqueline Kennedy Onassis Reservoir—is a unique New York City landmark in search of a future. Once a major element in the city's water supply system, the 106-acre basin between 86th and 96th streets is better known today for its jogging track, bird watching, peripheral landscaping and sweeping views of the city skyline.

Water from the Reservoir no longer flows through the city's pipes. The 1.5 billion gallons of water from upstate sources that its people use daily are now delivered chiefly by three underground tunnels. But fresh water is kept flowing into the Reservoir and—until its fate is decided—it is being carefully maintained as a scenic and wildlife attraction.

Most park visitors and long time parkgoers seem to agree that the Reservoir and its environs are at present in beautiful condition. But the historic body of water, the centerpiece of this large chunk of the park, is in the midst of an identity crisis. What will the future hold for this once-vital provider of water for the city's millions?

History of the Reservoir

Getting fresh water to New Yorkers has been a question of deep concern since the early 19th century. In the 1830s, the growing port city, crowded with newcomers from Europe, faced a major water crisis. Industrial

To the many New Yorkers and visitors who enjoy jogging, race walking or a leisurely stroll, the Central Park Reservoir is a calm oasis in the park. Birds, waterfowl and even an occasional turtle share the shoreline and spectacular views of the Manhattan skyline abound. Inset: The lower or receiving reservoir originally stretching from 79th to 85th streets was drained in 1930 and eventually transformed into the Great Lawn and Turtle Pond.

waste, a lack of sewers and ignorance of sanitation caused the pollution of many wells and sporadic outbreaks of cholera and yellow fever. Water from city wells was so unsafe, and public demand for a supply of fresh, clean water was so strong, that in 1837 construction began on a system of underground aqueducts, tunnels, piping and reservoirs that would carry water from the Croton River in upper Westchester county to the faucets of the city.

Construction was completed by 1842, and in the years that followed Croton water began to flow into private homes, fountains and public baths throughout the city. The system included a distributing reservoir located at Fifth Avenue and 42nd Street, and a bigger receiving reservoir, a stone rectangle stretching from 79th to 85th streets between Sixth and Seventh avenues that was later encompassed by Central Park. It was soon overshadowed by an even larger one to its immediate north, built between 1858 and 1862,

the Reservoir that embellishes the park today.

In the 20th century, the city's population expanded enormously, and a great demand for water required new ways of delivering it.

As distribution methods improved, the 42nd Street reservoir was deemed non-essential, then razed and replaced at the site by the New York Public Library in 1911. Two huge tunnels carrying water from the Delaware and Catskill reservoir systems were completed, the first in 1917, the second in 1937, and began to serve much of the city. No longer needed, the park's old receiving reservoir, sometimes called the lower reservoir, was removed from service and drained in 1930. A few years later, part of the empty pit was transformed into what is now called Turtle Pond and part was filled in and used to create the Great Lawn.

After that, the only surviving reservoir in the park was the one whose fate is now in question. Though a relic of the old Croton

system, for years it continued to supply tens of millions of gallons of water daily, and until the 1980s it was still servicing areas of Manhattan and The Bronx. But clearly, as work on a third water tunnel proceeded slowly but steadily, its days were numbered. After roughly 130 years of service, the Reservoir was disconnected from the water supply system in 1991.

Not very long after that, in August of 1998, a functioning section of the mammoth new tunnel was connected to distribution pipes in parts of the Bronx, Queens and Manhattan and began to supply water to those areas. City Tunnel No. 3 is not expected to be complete until around 2020, but its advent made it perfectly plain that never again would a section of Central Park be needed for a reservoir.

But what to do with the one we have, the largest single attraction in the park? That has been hotly debated, with advocates of increased recreational facilities such as ball fields, beaches, fishing piers, marinas and restaurants aligned against those who would keep the Reservoir fenced off as a wildlife habitat or converted into an open, natural-looking lake with minor recreational features.

Park officials and city political leaders, convinced that whatever course they choose will bring them plenty of abuse, appear to be in no rush to decide on a plan of action.

A Tour of the Reservoir

At most times of the year, a stroll around the Reservoir can be extremely pleasant. It is surrounded by a chain-link fence, erected to keep people from plunging in for a swim or tossing things into the water. Years ago, when the fence was lower, park employees in rowboats had to fish out objects such as lamps, guns, bicycle tires and—on one occasion—a complete set of the *Encyclopedia Britannica*. The 1.6 mile perimeter of the Reservoir is bordered by a cinder jogging track. Considered the busiest such track in the world, it is used each day by from 5000 to 10,000 runners, including an occasional celebrity.

The track and the adjacent bridle path are the best places for walkers to observe the gleaming expanse of water and its leafy setting. Although the Lake is the largest open body of water in the park, the enclosed Reservoir is far greater in size. Containing over a billion gallons of water at peak, it is half a mile across and occupies around one-eighth of the park's area. On its rim are two

Springtime along the western edge of the Reservoir reveals a fragrant path under flowering cherry trees.

tion for the avian species that frequent it. An excellent spot to observe the birds is along the north edge of the Reservoir. Great numbers of gulls, including ring-bills, herring gulls and black-backed gulls, inhabit its waters year-round. Mallard ducks, whose males flaunt lustrous green heads, are permanent residents; other ducks, including canvasbacks, ruddy ducks, shovelers, scaups, buffleheads and gadwalls, either stop off briefly or spend the winter.

Diving birds, including cormorants, loons, and pied-bill grebes, as well as wading birds like egrets and herons, also make short visits from time to time. They come to feed on the Reservoir's pickerel, carp, sunfish, and bass. Other birds feed on algae or the seeds from the grasses and weeds that are allowed to grow through the riprap of the Reservoir embankment.

At almost any point along the Reservoir's edge the views of city buildings towering beyond the tree line are admirable. But for pure visual enchantment and spectacular camera shots, the panoramic vista observable along its north shore is undoubtedly the best of all.

Rhododendron Mile

The terrain surrounding the Reservoir has long been known for its magnificent trees and flowering shrubs. But where, some visitors wonder, is the famous Rhododendron Mile we have heard about? The "mile" was actually a half-mile stretch along the East Drive, running parallel to the bridle path from near the southeast corner of the Reservoir at 86th Street to around 97th Street. In the early 1900s, its line of some 7000 rhododendron shrubs, a gift of Mrs. Russell Sage, was a spectacular sight as they burst into bloom in late spring. But over many decades, the plants suffered long periods of neglect and decline. As a result of recent restoration efforts, new rhododendrons have been planted in clusters inside the park entrance on Fifth Avenue just north of 85th Street and in scattered groups along the drive as far as 90th Street. In the words of Dennis Burton, the Conservancy's Chief Woodsman, "Continuation of the Rhododendron Mile restoration

fortress-like stone gatehouses, one on the south and the other on the north, built as stations for monitoring the amount and quality of the water. Today only the south gatehouse is staffed.

Between the two gatehouses runs a low stone wall, which neatly divides the Reservoir in two when the water is not high enough to cover it. This allows the closing off of one section at a time for cleaning. The water level has been kept low in recent years, and atop a length of the exposed wall a wooden walkway ending in a platform now reaches out into the water from the south gatehouse. This was built in the summer of 1998 as the site for a ceremony marking the activation of the third water tunnel, which burrows far below the Reservoir on its way to Queens and Brooklyn. Mayor Rudolph Giuliani also used the occasion to flip a switch reactivating an old fountain that sends five plumes of water, one for each of the city's boroughs, forty to sixty feet skyward from the surface in the southern end of the Reservoir.

Bird watchers, especially those interested in waterfowl, find the track the best place to use their binoculars. They regard the see-through fence not only as a way to keep the water clean but as protec-

awaits other donors."

Rhododendrons aside, a good way to enjoy some of the lavish plant life of the Reservoir vicinity—and a few other park attractions as well—is to wander along the bridle path. On the east side, a distinct highlight is the large number of ornamental cherry trees that line the area between the bridle path and the track from 87th Street northward. Some of the oldest were given to the park by Japan in 1912; others were presented later by Otto Marx, a prominent New Yorker. When the cherries blossom in April and May, this vicinity is one of the most pleasant in all the park.

Engineer's Gate

The area at Fifth Avenue and 90th Street, just inside Engineer's Gate, is sometimes the scene of intense activity. The drive at this point is the starting and sometimes finishing line of many of the footraces sponsored by the New York Road Runners Club. Visitors should note here the gilded bronze bust of John Purroy Mitchel to the west of the bridle path. A popular reform Mayor of New York, Mitchel died training for service in World War I. On the east side of the bridle path stands a brawny English elm, a tree with the third largest girth in the park and probably an original park planting. Another English elm, a knobby specimen west of the Mall at 70th Street, is usually considered the largest.

At 95th Street, a stroller who began at 86th will have travelled over

the longest straight path in the park. Although Olmsted and Vaux had a strong preference for curving walkways, the narrow corridor between the Reservoir and Fifth Avenue forced them to make all the paths and roads through it as straightaway as possible. Near 96th Street the bridle path turns westward around the top of the Reservoir and soon a truly majestic London plane

To play tennis in the park in the early 1880s required proper attire for both gentlemen and ladies. The game itself was a more genteel version than today's.

A horse and rider enjoy a quiet moment as they approach Gothic Bridge, where dappled sunlight plays on elegantly curving surfaces.

tree can be seen on the left. Impressively tall, possessed of the second biggest circumference, it is thought to be the oldest tree in the park.

After passing the two north gatehouse buildings, the path is spanned by an eye-catching cast-iron bridge, officially known as No. 28 but popularly called the Gothic Bridge. Another masterwork of Calvert Vaux, it has been celebrated for its graceful contours and distinctive ornamentation.

Tennis in the Park

The bridge connects the running track and the park's tennis courts, a fenced-in area with dozens of well-tended clay courts. Over objections of park purists, tennis was first permitted in 1884, on a meadow at the site of the present courts. They were paved in 1914, and in 1930 a tennis house was built. Once considered an upper-class sport, tennis has increased in popular appeal, as demonstrated by the wide range of people who buy permits to use these courts. Strollers find the tennis house a convenient place to stop for its restrooms, light refreshments or a bit of spectating.

The northwest stretch of the bridle path is another fine place for photography. As it turns down along the west side of the Reservoir, the path passes many tall turkey oaks intermingled with ornamental cherry and crab apple trees. Further along, the cherries predominate, and in spring the display of pink and white blossoms is stunning.

After curving leftward along the south of the Reservoir the path soon comes to another cast-iron bridge designed by Vaux. Called simply the Reservoir Bridge Southwest, it is notable for the floral ornamentation of the railings and spandrels. The bridge crosses from the running track to two paths, one to the west that leads over the 85th Street Transverse en route to the Pinetum, one to the east that takes you to the red brick buildings of the park's police precinct.

Further along to the east, the bridle path arrives at the South Gatehouse and the Southeast Reservoir Bridge. The smallest and least elegant of three cast-iron Reservoir spans designed by Vaux, it is by far the most trafficked, especially by joggers. The bridge links the running track with paths leading to the East Drive and to park entrances on Fifth Avenue.

NORTH QUADRANT

Central Park North (110th Street) to 97th Street

CENTRAL P

*Frederic
Douglass
Circle*

B,C

M10

109 St.

*Warrior's
Gate*

Playground

110th Street
Bridge

THE

Blockhouse
No. 1

108 St.
M10

SCALE
One city block
(north to south)
equals approximately
1/20th of a mile or
1/13th of a kilometer

107 St.

106 St.
M10

*Stranger's
Gate*

GREAT
HILL

105 St.

N

104 St.
M10

B,C

103 St.

W E S T

Glen Span Arch

Rustic Bridge
No. 30

102 St.
M10

THE
POOL

101 St.

P A R K

WEST DRIVE

100 St.
M10

*Boy's
Gate*

Soccer Field

Playground

C E N T R A L

97 St.

*All
Saints
Gate*

Rudin Family
Playground

B,C

96 St.

TRANSVERSES   **ROADWAYS**

• • • • • • •
BRIDLE PATHS

?

POLICE
CALL BOX   INFORMATION
DESK   PUBLIC
PHONE   FOOD
SERVICE   POLICE
STATION   RE
RO

Duke Ellington Circle

2,3

Farmer's Gate

Playground

Pioneer's Gate

M1,2,3,4

109 St.

Charles A. Dana Discovery Center

HARLEM MEER

M1,2,3,4

108 St.

Duck Island

Nutter's Battery Site

Walking Tour
page 96

Bernard Family Playground

107 St.

NORTH WOODS

Lasker Rink and Pool

McGown's Pass

Fort Clinton Site

M1,2,3,4, 106

106 St.

Huddlestone Arch

Fort Fish Site

Andrew Haswell Green bench

The Mount and McGown Tavern Site

Untermyer Fountain

105 St.

El Museo Del Barrio

Vanderbilt Gate Arsenal North

Conservatory Garden

WILDFLOWER MEADOW

COMPOSTING AREA

Burnett Memorial Fountain

104 St.

Museum of the City of New York

THE LOCH

THE RAVINE

Bridge

Bridge No.32

Dr. James Marion Sims

103 St.

M1,2,3,4, 106

Girl's Gate

102 St.

Soccer Field

Arthur Brisbane

101 St.

Springbanks Arch

EAST DRIVE

FIFTH

Soccer Field

Mount Sinai Medical Center

NORTH MEADOW

Playground

EAST MEADOW

Basketball and Handball Courts

North Meadow Recreation Center

M1,2,3,4, 106

98 St.

AVENUE

97 St.

97TH ST. TRANSVERSE

Albert Bertel Thorvaldsen

Woodmen's Gate 96 St.

MAP CONTINUED ON PAGE 86

M1,2,3,4,

| DIES ROOM | MEN'S ROOM | MEDICAL ASSISTANCE | PHOTO SITE | STATUE, MONUMENT | WATERFOWL SITE | BIRDING SITE | SUBWAY STATION | BUS STOP |

⊛ A Tour of the Meer

The second largest and to many the most appealing open body of water in the park, the Harlem Meer is the centerpiece of its northeast sector. The Meer and the terrain that circles it underwent a major restoration in the mid-1990s, and careful tending has kept the scenic, historic area in superb condition. A stone's throw from Duke Ellington Circle and just north of the Conservatory Garden, it is now one of the park's highlights and should not be missed.

The Meer, an eleven-acre mini-lake, was named after the Dutch word for "small sea." Like the larger rowboat lake in mid-park, it is an artificial creation, designed and built by Olmsted and Vaux to replace a tidal salt marsh and creek that covered the area. Once fed by Montayne's rivulet, the same stream used to create the Pool and the Loch, today most of the Meer's water is piped in from the Reservoir. Its average depth is four feet, but in some spots it reaches close to eight feet. Despite the tiny beach placed on its eastern shore, no swimming is allowed, as several large signs proclaim.

The banks of the Meer are interesting as well as comely. Richly endowed with magnificent trees, aquatic plant life and waterfowl, in places their paths branch up through clefts in the ancient bedrock to forts used in America's early wars. Standing on their shore-lines are two quite dissimilar structures, the Charles A. Dana Discovery Center and the Lasker Rink and Pool. For a rewarding look around the Meer, a walking tour is recommended.

Starting at the north gate of the Conservatory Garden, just off Fifth Avenue at 106th Street, the walkway leads onto a little flagstone terrace on the edge of the Meer's southeastern cove. Once a muddy backwater bordered by a concrete wall, it is now an attractive inlet lined with bayberry, swamp rose and blue flag iris. These and other plants were bedded along much of the shoreline for color and texture but also to provide food and shelter for the wildlife.

Moving up the eastern edge of the Meer, the pathway affords superb views of the shoreline, especially the rocky bluff rising above the south bank. This line of cliffs marked the northern limit of the park before it was extended from 106th to 110th Street in 1863, when the site the Meer now partially occupies was purchased. The east pathway also leads past some of the most spectacular trees in the park. Many are considered to be "Heritage Trees" because of their size or age, and some date to the early years of the park.

After passing some lofty red oaks and a brick concession stand, a stroller enters a grove of notable trees. Scattered on either side of the path, arboriphiles will find: distinc-

A view looking north across the Harlem Meer toward the Charles A. Dana Discovery Center. The building houses an information center for visitors and nature classes are held upstairs for children. Fishing poles can be rented to try your luck at catching (and then releasing) some of the 50,000 fish that were stocked when the Meer was restored in 1993.

tive horse chesnuts, which produce clusters of white flowers in the spring and prickly nut-filled pods in the fall; a venerable gray-barked European beech, whose lower trunk resembles a mammoth elephant's foot and whose nuts are relished by local squirrels and blue jays; century-old bald cypresses, moisture-loving trees usually found in swamplands like the bayous of Louisiana; statuesque Turkey oaks, native to western Asia and southern Europe, named after the country and not the bird; a graceful black-willow, a species commonly sighted along American rivers and whose black bark once was used in making gunpowder; and a group of grandly thriving ginkgos, an ancient species whose ancestors co-existed with dinosaurs 150 million years ago.

Across the path from the ginkgos, near a grassy place at the water's edge, a bronze plaque notes that the area is in memory of Cissy Patterson. Patterson, a journalist, was a benefactor of the Meer's restoration.

Continue along the path as it veers left onto the Meer's north bank. Nicely landscaped with wetland plants such as red maple and witch alder, the shoreline has been given a handsome cobblestone path that winds through the shrubbery to a stone terrace outside the Dana Center. With its panoramic view of the Meer, this is an excellent place for photographs or simply enjoying the sight.

Charles A. Dana Discovery Center

The Center itself is on the waterside site previously occupied by a boathouse, where rowboats could be rented and food purchased. By the early 1990s vandals had reduced it to ruins, a burnt-out wreck that had to be destroyed. During the restoration of the Meer, the current brick and wood building was erected. A playful combination of Victorian and alpine influences, it houses an excellent information room, with staffers on hand to answer questions or give directions, and a room overlooking the water that displays community projects and artwork. Nature classes are held upstairs for children, and anyone with photo identification can borrow a pole and bait for a bit of angling.

Fishing is not only permitted, it is encouraged, on a catch-and-release basis. The Meer was stocked in 1993 with 50,000 fish, including largemouth bass, channel catfish, golden shiners and bluegill and pumpkinseed sunfish. Asian grass carp were later added, because they feed on the algae that can cloud the water in warm summer months. An estimated 10,000 people a year try their luck, many of them casting lines from the open shoreline west of the Dana Center.

In the same general area, you will also see a grassy slope highly favored by ducks, geese and seagulls for socializing, sometimes with much honking and quacking. A bit further on, the path turns south along the west edge of the Meer into a stretch called the Locust Grove. This is a stand of some twenty century-old black locusts, notable for their furrowed bark and twisted trunks. In mid-spring they bear fragrant white blossoms, but in the fall they discard their seedpods, which can be poisonous if eaten. With their vaguely Asian appearance, these black locusts add a wonderfully scenic effect to the west bank of the Meer.

Lasker Rink and Pool

Just past the locust trees is the Lasker Rink, a place where many thousands happily skate in the winter and swim in the summer but which many others deplore as an architectural monster ill-suited to the area. Built in the 1950s, the rink displaced a portion of the Meer and an island in its southwest corner. During the restoration of the mid-1990s, a new island was built a short distance to the east to provide a habitat for the Meer's wildlife.

Called Duck Island, it has quickly become a familiar part of the landscape. Planted with pitch pine, bayberry, joe-pye weed and other native flora, it has formed a tangled thicket that attracts itinerant birds and year-round residents such as the whitethroated sparrow. Turtles and fish frequent the shoreline, and, true to its name, the island is a popular nesting place for the local Mallards and other waterfowl. Separated from predators like raccoons, unleashed dogs and human vandals, Duck Island seems to be flourishing.

Continuing along the curving south bank of the Meer, on the right rise rocky heights composed mainly of hard schist, the basic bedrock of Manhattan that was formed hundreds of millions of years ago. Indian trails and roads leading south to early New York City threaded their ways through the cliffs above the Meer. At strategic places, British and American troops built forts during the Revolutionary War and the War of 1812. Walking eastward, stone stairways on the right lead up to such historic sites as Nutter's Battery, McGown's Pass, Fort Fish and Fort Clinton (page 100).

Along the bench-lined shore, the path heads down the edge of the small southeastern cove. Fish like to shelter among the plant life there, which explains the frequent presence of children with fishing poles.

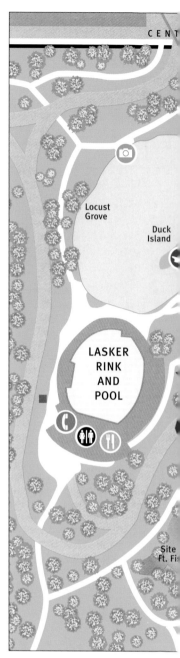

Conservatory Garden

One of the choicest of the park's crown jewels, the Conservatory Garden at Fifth Avenue and 105th Street is also one of its less frequented places. But the beautifully tended enclosure of plants, fountains and statuary, the only formal garden in the park, is a sensory experience that should not be missed.

The Vanderbilt Gate at the main entrance is itself an admirable sight. One of the finest examples of wrought iron work in New York City, it was made in France with designs by American architect George B. Post. The gate, which once adorned the mansion of Cornelius Vanderbilt II at Fifth Avenue and 58th Street, was given

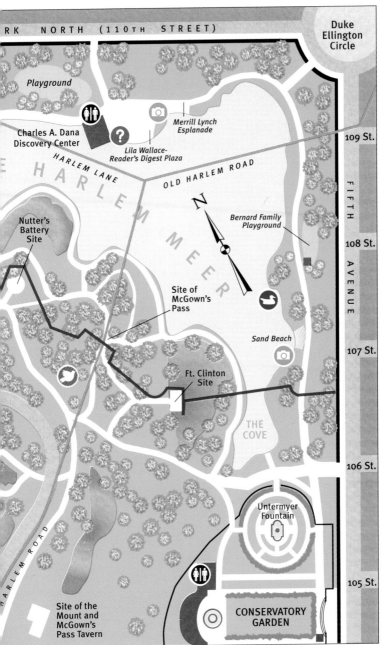

RK NORTH (110TH STREET)

Duke Ellington Circle

Playground

Charles A. Dana Discovery Center

Merrill Lynch Esplanade

Lila Wallace–Reader's Digest Plaza

HARLEM LANE

OLD HARLEM ROAD

109 St.

Nutter's Battery Site

HARLEM MEER

Bernard Family Playground

108 St.

FIFTH AVENUE

Site of McGown's Pass

Sand Beach

107 St.

Ft. Clinton Site

THE COVE

106 St.

Untermyer Fountain

105 St.

HARLEM ROAD

Site of the Mount and McGown's Pass Tavern

CONSERVATORY GARDEN

to the city by Gertrude Vanderbilt Whitney, founder of the Whitney Museum of American Art.

Inside the gate are six acres of wonderfully various plant life, including thousands of trees, shrubs, ferns, and a profusion of flowers ranging from rare old roses to the commonest of native wildflowers. Lining many sections of the grounds are hedges of English yew, barberry, Korean holly and Euonymus "Manhattan." This visual banquet is grouped within three distinct gardens. Each has its own character and charm.

The North Garden

This garden is arranged in a precise French style. At its center is the

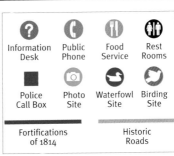

Information Desk	Public Phone	Food Service	Rest Rooms
Police Call Box	Photo Site	Waterfowl Site	Birding Site
Fortifications of 1814		Historic Roads	

Untermyer Fountain, whose pool is circled by *Three Dancing Maidens*, a delightful bronze by German sculptor Walter Schott. Surrounding the fountain are two concentric rings of flower beds. The interior one is used for "parterre," a highly ornamental arrangement of plant beds. The sloping outer ring is the stage for

Sites of America's Early Wars

One of the most intriguing areas in the park lies atop the bluffs south of the Harlem Meer. It is a forested region, full of winding paths, craggy promontories and places where some of America's early history was made.

In the days before the park was built, the lowland to the east below the bluffs was an impassable marshy tract that forced travelers to detour through a narrow gorge in the cliffs. This route, first an Indian trail and later used by the post roads coming to New York City from Albany and Boston in the 18th century, came to be called McGown's Pass after a family that owned a nearby tavern (page 106).

The scene of brisk military activity during the American Revolution and the War of 1812, this strategic passageway's main entry point was located where the stairway stands today in the cove of the Meer opposite the Dana Center, near lamppost #0726.

Defeated by the British in Brooklyn in August 1776, the Americans under George Washington withdrew to Manhattan, retreating across the future Central Park at the level of 94th Street and then north to Harlem Heights. By mid-September, pursuing British troops had seized the northern sector of the park, including McGown's Pass. In the ensuing Battle of Harlem Heights, the Americans repulsed the redcoats temporarily, but on October 16th Washington led his outgunned army out of Manhattan to White Plains and then New Jersey to continue the long fight for independence.

With the city in their hands, the British stationed a garrison of German mercenaries at McGown's Pass and erected a chain of fortifications across the Harlem bluffs to the shores of the Hudson. Bayonets, shot and other evidence of their military presence have been found in a number of places, including the park site known today as the Great Hill. These strongholds were held by the British until the war ended in 1783. On November 21st of that year, the German soldiers were withdrawn from McGown's Pass, and a few days later triumphant American troops under General Henry Knox marched through it on their way to New York City.

After that the pass was quiet for years, deserted except for the hunters in the surrounding forest and occasional travelers. But with the coming of the next conflict with the British, the War of 1812, city leaders grew fearful of an attack. The fear intensified after the British naval bombardment of Stonington, Connecticut, on August 10, 1814,

The gate and stockade at McGown's Pass was New York City's northern defense against the British during the War of 1812.

swarmed about this cluster of forts, armed with muskets or manning cannon, ready to defend Manhattan against the British. But the defenses were never put to the test. Before a shot was fired, the Treaty of Ghent was signed on December 24, 1814, putting an end to the war. By early 1815, the military posts were again abandoned, this time for good.

Today nothing remains of the fort at McGown's Pass, only a confluence of pathways where it stood at the level of 107th Street. But east of there, a path winds its way to the site of Fort Clinton, perched on the edge of a promontory overlooking the eastern shore of the Meer. Built on a spot occupied by the British during the Revolutionary war, the fort was named after DeWitt Clinton, the Mayor of New York in 1814. Standing today at its semicircular iron railing and viewing the scene spread out below, visitors can easily imagine the damage its guns would have done to a force advancing toward the bluffs. For years, a cannon and mortar were in place at the fort, but they and a bronze plaque relating some of the fort's history had to be removed due to vandalism.

Of all the structures built to defend the bluffs in 1814 only one actually remains standing, Blockhouse No. 1. The oldest building in the park, this rugged stone structure stands on the edge of a high precipice called "The Cliff" in its forested northwest sector (page 109).

making it seem possible that enemy ships would ferry troops across Long Island Sound and invade the city from the north.

A call went out for volunteers to rebuild the fortifications along the bluffs, and within days an army of civilians, including students from Columbia College, firemen, lawyers, and members of the Master Butchers Association and the Sons of Erin, was working night and day to build a cordon of outposts stretching from Third Avenue to the Hudson River. They fortified McGown's Pass, building a thick wooden barrier gate surmounted by a blockhouse and flanked by cannon. They also erected Fort Clinton to the east and Nutter's Battery to the west, then formed a strong defense line by linking both to the fort at the pass with an earthen breastwork. On higher ground to the south, the volunteers built Fort Fish, the largest, most heavily armed of the strongholds above the Meer.

For a time, some 1600 militiamen

Fort Fish at the time of the War of 1812

dazzling seasonal displays: 20,000 tulips in the spring, and 2000 chrysanthemums in the fall. Over the four entryways to the garden's center are arbors of climbing "Silver Moon" roses, which produce gleaming white (and a few pink-tinted) flowers in June.

The Central Garden

Influenced by classic Italian gardens, this one includes a luxuriant lawn, an unadorned fountain with a single graceful jet, and an ornate wrought iron arbor covered with Chinese wisteria. It is truly magnificent in the spring, when the arbor is covered with hanging violet and purple clusters and the crab apple trees along two nearby walkways flaunt their pink and white blossoms. The stairways flanking the fountain lead up to a walk under the arbor, where visitors can view the garden below and Fifth Avenue buildings rising in the background.

The South Garden

Designed in a more relaxed English style, this is perhaps the most popular of the three. In the center of its artfully diverse assortment of flower beds, shrubs, trees and hedges is a statuary fountain memorializing Frances Hodgson Burnett, writer of the classic children's book, *The Secret Garden*. Sculpted by Bessie Potter Vonnoh, the bronze statue shows a reclining boy playing a flute while a young girl, holding a water basin, stands listening. The pedestal rises from a picturesque pool, and in spring and summer the area is scented by magnolia, perfumed Japanese lilac trees and *Nicotiana*, a relative of the tobacco plant. It is a lovely place, favored by painters, photographers and garden fanciers.

The botanical arts were very much on the agenda of Olmsted and Vaux. Their plans for a large Conservatory at 72nd Street and Fifth Avenue failed to materialize, but a plant nursery was established at the site of the present garden soon after the park opened. Under the supervision of the park's head gardener, the talented Ignaz Pilat (page 71), it had a heated greenhouse ninety-four feet long and a smaller propagating house. Judging by official accounts, Pilat and his crew cultivated many thousands of specimens, including trees, that were later planted in the park.

In 1899, a splendid, multi-sectioned glass Conservatory was erected in the same locale. The largest municipal conservatory in the country, it presented opulent seasonal floral displays and became one of the city's major showplaces. Its Easter flower show, for example, was a highly popular annual event in the early part of the 20th century. In 1901, more than 1.4 million people came to see the chrysanthemum exhibit in the fall.

Though the Conservatory had public appeal as well as a practical horticultural function, it was also costly to maintain. In the Depression year of 1934, it was torn down, presumably as a cost-cutting measure. Three years later, on the very same spot, the newly created

Three Dancing Maidens, *sculpted by Walter Schott, circle the Untermyer Fountain, centerpiece of the North Garden. Seasonal displays of tulips and chrysanthemums are bordered by crab apple trees and lilac bushes.*

Bessie Potter Vonnoh sculpted this fountain pair to commemorate Frances Hodgson Burnett, author of The Secret Garden. *The boy plays his pipe to attract birds while the girl offers them a bowl of water to drink from.*

South Garden became known as the mystery of the vanishing rue anemones, white-flowered members of the buttercup family. For a time, no one could understand why they kept disappearing from the flower beds. Then it was learned that the Botanical Garden in the Bronx had the same problem. The answer to the puzzle seems to be that the plant is used in voodoo rituals and that its power is intensified if it is stolen. Needless to say, rue anemone is no longer planted at the Conservatory Garden.

Today, the Conservatory Garden is fastidiously maintained and vigilantly guarded. Though not a place that rivals, or wishes to rival, the Zoo or the Terrace in crowd appeal, it remains a favorite with Central Park cognoscenti and others drawn to its quiet beauty. Teachers bring groups of young schoolchildren to the appealing, semi-enclosed area near the Burnett fountain for story-telling sessions. The lawn of the Central Garden is in demand for weddings, and the stairways leading up to the wisteria arbor are a popular spot for wedding photos. Permission to hold weddings can be arranged by calling (212) 360-2766. The Conservatory Garden is open daily from 8 a.m. until dusk. Free tours start at the front gate Saturday at 11 a.m., April - October.

The Loch

Can this really be Manhattan? First time visitors to the Loch and its woodland setting can be forgiven for wondering. Starting below the cascade at the northeast tip of the Pool, this suprisingly sylvan habitat seems a world away from the sidewalks of New York.

A path to the right of the little cascade soon leads to the Glen Span Arch, a massive gray stone structure that serves as a gateway to the area. Beyond the arch, the forest dominates. A stroller follows the rock-lined stream through the woods to an oval where paths converge. Tall

Conservatory Garden was opened to the public.

Like the rest of the park, it experienced periods of budget-slashing, maintenance cutbacks and general neglect. But things picked up significantly in the 1930s when the Conservancy began to generate large amounts of private funding and a general restoration was started at the garden. A full-time gardener was hired. Long neglected trees and hedges were pruned, 20,000 square feet of turf were resodded and the North Garden acquired thousands of new bulbs and plants. The "woodland slope" along the back of the garden was replanted with over a hundred kinds of ferns, perennials, and wildflowers.

In the South Garden, the vandalized Burnett Memorial Fountain was repaired. The boy's arm and flute, the girl's hand, and a bird had been broken off and stolen. Sculptor John Terken remodeled the lost parts, had them cast in Italy and restored them to the statue.

Another case of vandalism in the

In the Center Garden, the graceful jet of a single fountain punctuates alternating hedges of dark yew and light-green spiraea beneath the wisteria pergola.

The colors of spring are richly varied in the South Garden, where Conservatory gardeners have created a masterful composition in subtle shades of rose, blue and purple. A Japanese lilac tree and a single spear of foxglove provide sparkling white accents.

Carefree Winds roses blooming in the North Garden. Roses of many varieties and hues grace its outer flower beds and arbors in the late spring and summer.

May is a special time in the Conservatory Garden with lush cascades of wisteria hanging from terrace railings adjacent to the ornate pergola.

Thousands of pink and red tulips in the North Garden create a dazzling spring display. In the fall, brilliant chrysanthemums fill the same beds.

The Mount: Convent, Tavern, Art Museum and Compost Heap

Although it has a rich and varied past, the area known as The Mount is most notable these days as the site of the park's chief composting operation, a place where leaves and branches are recycled into useful plant food. Yet there is one visible reminder of a far different time: the remnant of an old foundation wall that often stirs the curiosity of visitors. Who made this venerable wall and when? And why is this modest elevation referred to as The Mount?

Before the park was built, people traveling to and from New York City would stop for rest and refreshment at taverns in the rural vicinity of Harlem. The earliest, Jansen's Half Way House,

was built in 1684 somewhere around the present 109th Street. The old wall at the mulching site dates to about 1750, when it was part of the foundation of a tavern built there by Jacob Dyckman. It evidently was a sizable structure, since the Colonial Assembly met there in 1752. The Dyckman family sold it in 1759 to Catherine McGown, widow of a Scottish sea captain, and the nearby road soon came to be called McGown's Pass. She and her descendants operated the tavern until the 1840s.

The property began a new chapter in 1847, when it was purchased by the Sisters of Charity of St. Vincent de Paul and soon transformed into a vigorous religious community they called Mount St. Vincent. By the mid-1850s it counted among its numbers seventy sisters, housed a boarding academy for two hundred "young ladies," ran a free

McGown's Pass Tavern was a favorite watering spot for gentlemen after a day's riding—or racing—in the park.

:chool for children who lived
·earby, and included a substan-
al brick chapel and refectory.

In 1858 the New York State
·gislature approved the acquisi-
on of land for Central Park, and
vo years later the sisters had to
·ave the Mount. They moved to
ie Bronx, where the convent
nd school still thrive.

For a time, the buildings they
acated were used by the park
ommissioners for offices, but
uring the Civil War from 1861 to
865 they were made into mili-
iry hospitals and the sisters
eturned temporarily to nurse the
/ounded. After the war, the old
/ooden building became a tavern
gain, while the chapel was
·ansformed into a statue gallery
lled with plaster casts of the
/orks of Thomas Crawford, an
minent American sculptor of
ie period.

As the decades passed, the tav-
·rn became the haunt of politi-
ians and wealthy sportsmen like
'illiam H. Vanderbilt and August
·elmont. "In the evenings,"
/rote social historian Lloyd
1orris, "it was left to the patron-
ge of gentlemen of rakish tastes
nd their abandoned feminine
ompanions." After a fire in 1881
estroyed the Mount St. Vincent
uildings, a new and even
rander tavern was erected
espite the objections of temper-
nce groups. At the request of
he Sisters of Charity, the man-
gers of the enterprise removed
ll reference to Mount St. Vincent
nd revived the older name of
1cGown's Pass Tavern.

At the turn of the century and
fter, the tavern was a fashion-
ble destination for well-to-do
1anhattanites. For years the pro-
·rietor awarded a magnum of
hampagne to the first sleigh to
each the tavern after the sea-
on's first snow. It was open every
ay of the year, and the music,
ancing and general revelry last-
d until the early hours of the
norning. But in the years prior to
Vorld War I, its popularity began
o wane. In 1915, the city ousted
he lessee of the property and
uctioned off all its sporting
rints, oil paintings and other
elics. Even "Old Gabe," the
ostelry's aged parrot, was sold
or $45.00. In 1917, the tavern
/as torn down.

trees are everywhere, and within
the oval stand two mighty red oaks
probably old enough to have been
there before the park was built.

To the left a rustic log bridge
crosses above another cascade to a
path that runs parallel to the water-
way through beautifully wooded
terrain on the western slope. The
forested areas on both sides of the
ravine are officially known as the
North Woods, and a large sign
informs visitors that it is a "protect-
ed New York City Ecosystem where
no bicycles or unleashed dogs are
permitted."

Instead of taking the bridge
route, go right at the oval, then
right again at the creek trickling
from the south. This takes you to
the secluded Springbanks Arch, an
engaging little stone span that must
be the least known of all the arches
Calvert Vaux designed for the park.

Backtracking along the creek,
take the path that crosses another
rustic bridge and then turns northward along the eastern bank of the
Loch. Named by Olmsted with the
Scottish word for lake, it once was a
much more substantial body of
water. Although years of siltation
and general neglect have narrowed
the Loch considerably, work has
been done in recent years to imbed
new wetland plants and improve
the stream's flow.

After passing some large fallen
trees along the bank, a visitor will
notice a number of dirt trails leading down to the water's edge. Some
have been made by bird watchers.
During the spring migration, many
come each morning to find spots in
the thicket along the stream to peer
through their binoculars at the
frenzy of avian activity. On the
other side of the paved path, the
slopes are studded with handsome
trees, and after a log railing appears
it is possible to glimpse through the
trees the fenced edges of the wildflower meadow. Thanks to a donation from the Garden Club of
America, this hillside area is planted
with a fascinating variety of native
grasses and wildflowers. It is highly
popular with butterflies, bees and
hummingbirds. To reach it, take the
next right and go up the hill.

As the path comes to the end of
the Loch, it slants down to the edge
of still another pleasant little cascade. Here a bridge made of boulders crosses the water to a stone
stairway leading to the western
slopes of the ravine. The Loch flows

ahead through the Huddlestone Bridge, on its way under the Lasker Rink and finally into the Meer.

Huddlestone Arch

The Huddlestone itself is one of the highlights of a visit to the Loch. It is not only the most picturesque of all the park's archways but one of its most impressive structures. Made entirely of rough boulders, one weighing 100 tons, it was fitted together without binding material of any sort. It has stood since 1866 thanks solely to the force exerted by gravity and friction on properly wedged stones, and people have been known to hurry through it when they learn how it was built. But the Huddlestone carries the East Drive over the Loch, and it has proven its sturdiness by withstanding the traffic change from carriages to automobiles and not ever needing repair. A marvel of construction, it is also a thing of curious beauty, particularly in spring when yellow forsythia drapes over its mammoth dark stones.

The Pool

No question about it, the little body of water called the Pool has a romantic appeal. Its banks are lined with beautiful weeping willows and other magnificent trees and its waters and reeds are graced by a large population of waterfowl. This charming place is one of the highlights of the upper park.

Although the Pool and its setting seem quite natural, they were in fact creations of Olmsted, Vaux and their team of park-builders. They made the Pool by damming Montayne's Rivulet, a stream that ran through the area, before sending it along on a northeastward course to help form the Loch and finally the Meer. Over the years, the stream's natural flow from Manhattan's West Side was disrupted by residential and commercial construction, and today the water that tumbles so prettily from a rocky cavern into the Pool has been piped there from the Reservoir.

The impressive variety of shrubs, flowers and trees on the turf surrounding the Pool is also a tribute to

the landscaper's art. In a circuit of its modest 1.5 acre expanse, a visitor will find superb specimens of indigenous northeastern trees such as the sycamore, hickory, maple and locust, as well as decorative nonnative types like the bald cypress from the southern swamps and the Osage orange from Oklahoma.

Along the path on the south shore is the little cavern where water splashes down into the Pool. A few paces further on, a small peninsula on the left curves out into the water. This is a fine spot to take pictures, feed the ducks or admire the colorful mix of foliage on the opposite bank.

To finish exploring the Pool go left across the brown wooden bridge to the north shore. Take the path heading back toward the park entrance. It leads you past some exceptional individual trees, including a statuesque American sycamore, a robust red maple, brilliant in the fall, and finally to a small group of Osage oranges whose grainy, inedible green fruit hang like ornaments. This stretch of the shoreline is also a notable example of the deft landscaping of Olmsted and Vaux. To the right of the path, between it and the park's peripheral wall, they built the steep slope and planted the shrubbery and tall trees that still prevent many of the sights and sounds of Central Park West from intruding too boldly into the Pool's tranquil realm.

Blockhouse No. 1

Of all the structures built to defend the bluffs in 1814 only one actually remains standing, Blockhouse No. 1. The oldest building in the park, this rugged stone structure stands on the edge of a high precipice called "The Cliff" in its forested northwest sector. Once it had a sunken wooden roof with a mobile cannon that could be deployed quickly to fire in any direction over the parapet. Today the Blockhouse is empty, roofless and securely locked.

Although numerous paths lead to the old stronghold, it is an isolated area and attracts far fewer people than the forts above the Meer. Solitary wandering there is not advisable. Still, if a group visit can be arranged, a close look at the Blockhouse and its stunning cliffside location can be rewarding.

*The Pool mirrors the brilliant fall
foliage of the bankside trees.*

SPORTS IN THE PARK

Jogging

Central Park is a jogger's paradise. Every day thousands of them take to the cinder path around the Reservoir or to the pavement of the drives. Lengths of various running routes are indicated on the adjoining map. Lanes on the drives are marked off for joggers, but they use the entire road when automobile traffic is closed off (daily between 10 a.m. and 3 p.m. and after 7 p.m.; weekends from 7 p.m. Friday to 6 a.m. Monday).

Most joggers do it for fun or fitness, but some are training for one of the races or group runs staged in the park by the New York Road Runners Club. The frequently-held events range from races of a few miles to the annual New York Marathon. For information or to join the club, call (212) 860-4455. A word of caution: jogging alone at night or pre-dawn is never advisable.

Biking & Skating

Biking is permitted only on the park drives, not on the walkways. Best times are when cars are off the road (see above). Bikes can be rented next to the Boathouse at 74th Street and the East Drive. For rental information, call (212) 861-4137. Inline skaters also use the drives, but many find the spaces on the north end of the Mall and the closed driveway to the west of the Mall to be more suitable. Inline skating is available at Wollman Rink, April through September. For hours and rental information, call (212) 396-1010.

Tennis

The park's fenced-in tennis area, located on the northwest of the Reservoir, has thirty well-tended courts. Permits, required much of the year, can be obtained in the basement of the Arsenal. For fees and other details, call (212) 360-8131.

Ice Skating and Swimming

Ice skating is extremely popular at the Wollman Rink and the Lasker Rink, from November through March. For hours and rental information at Wollman, call (212) 396-1010; for Lasker, call (212) 534-7639. Lasker also has a swimming season in July and August, when lessons are available. No swimming is permitted in any of the park's open bodies of water.

Baseball/Softball

Baseball diamonds on the North Meadow have been undergoing restoration but are scheduled to reopen in the spring of 2000. Seven softball fields are located on the Great Lawn, five on the Heckscher Ballfields. Permits are obtainable at Arsenal West, 16 West 61st Street; call (212) 408-0226.

Rowing/Fishing

Rowing on the Lake is one of the park's greatest pleasures. Boats are rented at the booth next to the Boathouse. A gondola can be rented by the half hour in the evenings. For information, call (212) 517-2233. Fishing is a touchy subject. The only place it is actively encouraged is the Harlem Meer, which has been stocked with thousands of fish. Bait and poles are available free at the Dana Discovery Center; the fishing policy is "catch and release." Fishing on the Lake is tolerated, but lead sinkers have poisoned a number of birds, including a young swan, and there is some demand for stiffer regulation of the fisherfolk.

Horseback Riding

The park has a long and scenic bridle path. Riders rent or board their mounts at the Claremont Riding Academy, 175 West 89th Street. The oldest and largest such establishment in New York, it offers private and class lessons. For information, call (212) 724-5100.

Soccer

Soccer playing on lawn areas is frowned upon, though ad hoc matches are common on the East Meadow and in Rumsey Playfield. When the North Meadow reopens in 2000, it will have soccer fields, for which permits will be issued at Arsenal West.

Lawn Bowling and Croquet

Exquisitely-tended green lawns north of the Sheep Meadow near the West Drive are home grounds to the mannerly old sports of lawn bowling and croquet. Lessons are available for beginners. For information about using the facilities, drop by the greens on a weekend or call the New York Lawn Bowling Club at either (212) 289-3245 or (212) 877-4147.

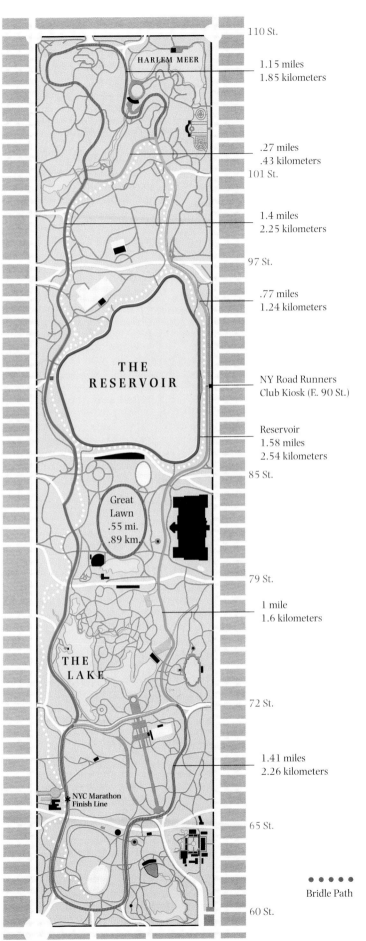

110 St.

HARLEM MEER

1.15 miles
1.85 kilometers

.27 miles
.43 kilometers

101 St.

1.4 miles
2.25 kilometers

97 St.

.77 miles
1.24 kilometers

THE
RESERVOIR

NY Road Runners
Club Kiosk (E. 90 St.)

Reservoir
1.58 miles
2.54 kilometers

85 St.

Great
Lawn
.55 mi.
.89 km.

79 St.

1 mile
1.6 kilometers

THE
LAKE

72 St.

1.41 miles
2.26 kilometers

NYC Marathon
Finish Line

65 St.

• • • • •
Bridle Path

60 St.

BIRD SPOTTING IN THE PARK

Central Park, situated on the path of two major migration flyways, has been an oasis for birds and birders since its earliest days. Today the park is rated by ornithologists as one of the country's major bird-watching locales, and in 1996 a total of 275 species were seen within its borders. A sample of this rich variety is shown here.

The spring and fall migrations are peak times for spotting birds and trying to identify them. A pair of binoculars, some decent walking shoes and a field guide to the birds are all you need. Early morning is usually the best time, and do not hesitate to ask the park's regular birders for advice. These friendly, knowledgeable enthusiasts can show you where the action is on any particular day.

In March, grackles and robins begin to appear, followed by a major avian invasion in April and May. Among the pack are thrushes, herons, hummingbirds, kingbirds, many kinds of warblers, and brightly-colored orioles, tanagers, grosbeaks and indigo buntings. They can be seen in many parts of the park, but the best spots are on the Bow Bridge over the center of the Lake, the woodsy areas along the Loch and a number of sites in the Ramble, including the Point, the Azalea Pond and the rocks overlooking the Lake.

Many birds are passing through, others stay the summer. The fall migration, starting in late September, brings nuthatches, chickadees, and great numbers of waterbirds, including ruddy ducks, scaups and mergansers, to join the resident mallards and gulls. Good places to watch for these species are the Pool, the Pond, the Lake, the Meer and the Reservoir. The fall also brings passing chevrons of geese, ill-defined flights of cormorants and large numbers of travelling hawks, all of which can be viewed best from the upper levels of Belvedere Castle. When the fall migration ends, the park is left to such year-round denizens as sparrows, jays, titmice and cardinals.

For specifics about bird watching in the park, visit the information center at Belvedere Castle or call (212) 772-0210.

Female

Wood Duck
Aix sponsa
17 - 20 in. long

Green-winged Teal
Anas crecca
13 - 16 in. long

Male

Female

Male

Ruddy Duck
Oxyura jamaicensis
14 - 16 in. long

Female

Male

Canvasback
Aythya valisineria
19 - 24 in. long

Herring Gull
Larus argentatus
22 - 26 in. long

Great Egret
Casmerodius albus
37 - 41 in. long

Black-crowned Night-Heron
Nycticorax nycticorax
23 - 28 in. long

Double-crested Cormorant
Phalacrocorax auritus
29 - 36 in. long

Female

Male

American Black Duck
Anas rubripes
21 - 25 in. long

Bufflehead
Bucephala albeola
13 - 16 in. long

Female

Male

Mallard
Anas platyrynchos
20 - 28 in. long

American Crow
Corvus brachyrynchos
17-21 in. long

European Starling
Sturnus vulgaris
7 - 8 1/2 in. long

Common Grackle
Quiscalus quiscu
10-12 1/2 in. long

Blue Jay
Cyanocitta cristata
11-12 1/2 in. long

Northern Mockingbird
Mimus polyglotto
9 -11 in. long

Downy Woodpecker
Picoides pubescens
6 -7 in. long

Male

Female

Male

Femal

House Finch
Carpodacus mexicanu
5 - 5 1/2 in. lon

Female

Male

Song Sparrov
Melospiza melodi
5 - 7 in. lon

House Sparrow
Pusser domesticus
5 - 6 in. long

Female

Yellow Warbler
Dendroica petechia
4 1/2 - 5 1/2 in. long

Male

Golden-crowned Kinglet
Regulus satrapa
3 1/4 - 4 1/4 in. long

Red-tailed Hawk
Buteo jamaicensis
19-26 in. long

Male

Female

Red-winged Blackbird
Agelaius phoenicius
7 - 9 1/2 in. long

Male

Female

Northern Cardinal
Cardinalis cardinalis
7 1/2 - 8 1/2 in. long

Mourning Dove
Zenaida macroura
10 - 12 in. long

American Robin
Turdus migratorius
9 - 11 in. long

115

Flowering cherries form a pale pink canopy of color over the bridle path along the east side of the Reservoir in the spring.

CALENDAR OF BLOOM TIMES

Cooler winters or warmer springs may delay or quicken the blooming of different species, usually by no more than a week. The adjoining map indicates some of the good places in the park to see favorite blooms; but you may also find them in other, unexpected places.

Mid-Late March
First to be seen are the **crocuses, snowdrops** and fragrant **honeysuckle**, all of which appear in many areas of the park. The delicate yellow of the **Cornelian cherry trees** begins to brighten the scenery, a prelude to the coming host of golden **daffodils**.

A large stand of forsythia flowers atop Cherry Hill and adjacent to the newly restored fountain.

A sure sign of spring, many thousands of them delight winter-weary eyes along pathways and on lawns and hillsides. Next come the magnificent yellow **forsythia**, and the first of the **magnolias** start to show their pink and white blooms.

Early April
As the **magnolias** continue their display, and **daffodils** continue to reign, they are joined by multi-colored little **scilla blossoms** and **flowering quince**. This native of Japan, which bears orange and scarlet flowers, is the shrub that forms one of the handsome hedges in the Conservatory Garden. By now, the **sassafras** trees in the Ramble are showing clusters of yellow-green flowerets. The **Callery pear** trees also are flaunting their bonny white blossoms, and a good place to see them is the Grand Army Plaza. Around this time of year the plaza is—or soon will be—ablaze with yellow, white and red spring flowers.

Mid-April
"Loveliest of trees, the cherry now/Is hung with bloom along the bough." As the poem promises, around the third week of April some of the **cherry trees** along the east edge of the Reservoir begin to show their comely white blossoms. This is also the time when legions of **tulips** add their red and yellow splendor to many parts of the park. Sweet-smelling **hyacinths** enliven the palette with their purples, whites and pinks. Shrubs like **shadbush** and **viburnum** are dotted with white blooms, and **shepherd's purse, dan-**

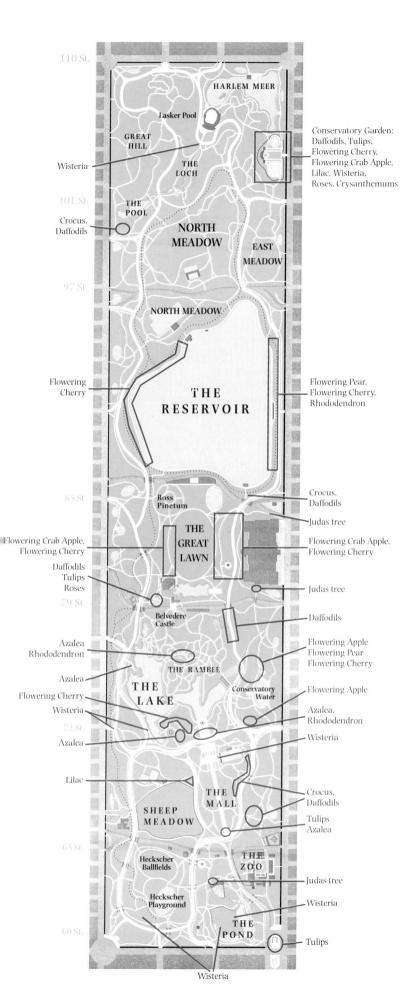

110 St.

HARLEM MEER

Lasker Pool

GREAT HILL

THE LOCH

Conservatory Garden: Daffodils, Tulips, Flowering Cherry, Flowering Crab Apple, Lilac, Wisteria, Roses, Crysanthemums

Wisteria

101 St.

THE POOL

Crocus, Daffodils

NORTH MEADOW

97 St.

EAST MEADOW

NORTH MEADOW

Flowering Cherry

THE RESERVOIR

Flowering Pear, Flowering Cherry, Rhododendron

85 St.

Ross Pinetum

Crocus, Daffodils

Judas tree

THE GREAT LAWN

Flowering Crab Apple, Flowering Cherry

Flowering Crab Apple, Flowering Cherry

Daffodils Tulips Roses

Judas tree

79 St.

Belvedere Castle

Daffodils

Azalea Rhododendron

Flowering Apple Flowering Pear Flowering Cherry

THE RAMBLE

Azalea

THE LAKE

Conservatory Water

Flowering Cherry

Flowering Apple

Wisteria

Azalea, Rhododendron

72 St.

Azalea

Wisteria

Lilac

Crocus, Daffodils

THE MALL

SHEEP MEADOW

Tulips Azalea

65 St.

Heckscher Ballfields

THE ZOO

Heckscher Playground

Judas tree

Wisteria

60 St.

THE POND

Tulips

Wisteria

delion, wild geranium, violets and other wildflowers have arrived in great abundance.

Late April

All the **flowering cherries**, along both the east and west edges of the Reservoir, on the periphery of the Great Lawn, on Cherry Hill and elsewhere, are

The redbud or Judas tree with its distinctive pale purple blooms is seen here in a late spring display.

now in their full pink and white glory. The **dogwoods** also are in bloom, along the shores of the Turtle Pond and the Lake as well in the Conservatory Water area, to name but a few sites. Long-awaited, hundreds of blossoming **crab apple** trees ornament drives and pathways throughout the park. Two superb allées of crab apples at the Conservatory Garden are just one of its many springtime attractions. In Wagner Cove, at the south end of the Mall, near the pond in the center of the Ramble and in many other parts of the park, orange, red, pink and white **azaleas** begin to bloom, as do the first **lilacs**.

Early May

This is a good time to visit the Singer Lilac Walk along the northeast corner of the Sheep Meadow. There many expertly-tended species of purple, pink and white **lilacs**, including some from Europe and Asia, combine to provide a visual and aromatic banquet. Along the bridle path just east of the Reservoir and flanking the stairways at Bethesda

Terrace, the **rhododendrons** also are in bloom, showing off their own purples, pinks and whites. **Wisteria**, the beautiful vine from Asia, is sending cascades of purple blossoms down from pergolas east of the Mall and in the central garden of the Conservancy Garden as well as from arbors in the west seventies. Elsewhere, handsome **Horse Chestnuts** are in blossom, their branches carrying upright clusters of white flowers.

Mid-May

More trees, including the **mountain ash** and the **black and honey locusts**, have produced their flowery clusters. **Chinese dogwood** is in bloom. The tall, stately **tulip trees** (yellow poplars), including four near the Pool and one venerable specimen on the path leading down to the north entrance to the Loch, also bloom in late May. Their flowers are large, fragrant and tulip-like, a striking orange and green, but they blossom on branches so high in the tree that they are near impossible to see— unless the wind shakes one down to the ground. In many areas, yellow

Flowering azaleas on Cherry Hill reach their peak in May.

and purple **iris** are plentiful, as are such wildflowers as **Queen Anne's lace, nightshade,** and **clover.**

June

Roses blooming in every imaginable shade are the highlight of the month. The Shakespeare Garden, to the west of Belvedere Castle, has some pretty specimens among its fascinating collection of plants. The Conservatory Garden has rare and beautiful varieties. In the Loch, pale pink swamp roses are in bloom on the shrubby island in

Rhododendrons at Bethesda Terrace in May

the stream, while the multiflora rose shows its small white flowers in the Ramble and other informal places. The park's few dozen **catalpa** trees display large bell-shaped flowers, a dazzling white with orange stripes and purple spots. Near mid-month, the tiny flowers of the **linden trees** perfume the air through many areas of the park. Rare **Chinese scholar trees** in the Ramble and south of the Pond carry cream-colored clusters of flowers. Many shrubs, including **mountain laurel, cotoneaster, privet, sumac,** and **Japanese holly** are in bloom.

July

Some plants are fruiting, and the number of new bloomings has declined. In the Ramble, the **bottle-brush buckeye** shrubs begin to show clusters of yellow-green flowers, which sometimes have an unpleasant odor. The intriguingly named **euonymous Manhattan,** shaped into hedges in the Conservatory Garden, is in blossom. The attractive shrub is, incidentally, named for the city of Manhattan, Kansas. Other bloomings over the month vary from **day lilies** and **bee balm,** to **joe-pye weed, chicory, coneflowers** and **black-eyed Susans.** The last two are daisy-like, with yellow, purple or orange rays and black or brown centers.

August

Again more fruiting than blooming is going on. The small prickly tree known variously as **Hercules club,** **Devil's walking stick** or the **angelica tree,** displays large creamy white flowers. The **cardinal flower** sends out brilliant red spikes. Some **chrysanthemums,** a highly popular late-blooming species that flourishes in the fall, may flower late in August.

September

In the woodsy areas of the park, the later weeks of this month bring the fall blossoming of the wonderful **witch hazel shrub** and its slender-petaled yellow flowers. Highly useful, the plant is used to make a soothing, astringent lotion. Its branches have been thought by some to be effective as divining rods in searching for underground water or minerals. Also gracing the woods, as well as slopes along the driveways, are slender wands of yellow **goldenrod.** It was once erroneously believed to be a cause of hay fever, perhaps because it blooms at the same time as the real culprit, the less conspicuous **ragweed.** Goldenrod leaves traditionally have been used in medicinal preparations and teas. The **white wood aster,** a common wildflower in the park, becomes plentiful this month in the Loch and Ramble. It blooms in flat-topped clusters of dainty white flowers with daisy-like ray petals. The stems and leaves of the white aster once were used as a seasoning in Native American cooking. Other aster varieties, including some with pink, blue or purple flowers, bloom somewhat later in the year.

TREES IN THE PARK

Central Park is well known for the abundance and variety of its trees. According to the most recent survey,* it has about 25,000 individual trees over six inches in diameter, and many smaller ones. They belong to 148 species and many of these have been clearly labeled by the Conservancy so that budding arborists and visitors can identify the varieties.

In creating beautifully wooded terrain from a near-wasteland, the builders of Central Park stressed variety. The mid-19th century was a period of intense American interest in horticulture and in plant material from all over the world. Olmsted especially was eager to plant exotic (non-native) trees, and almost half of the 334 species originally planted in the park were of foreign origin. Many did not survive, and others, like the fertile ailanthus ("tree of heaven"), are now regarded as undesirable weeds. Current thinking at most parks, including Central Park, is to emphasize planting native trees but not to exclude totally the "non-invasive" exotics.

According to the survey, the park has a number of unusual trees, including the Kentucky coffee tree, cucumber magnolias, atlas cedars and metasequoias, also called dawn redwoods, once thought to have

The 1982 Central Park Tree Inventory

become extinct sixty million years ago.

The most numerous species in the park is the black cherry, followed by the American elm and pin oak. An English elm west of the Mall at 68th Street, with a breast-high circumference of over seventeen feet, is the tree with the largest trunk; a London plane on the north of the Reservoir is second with a girth of sixteen feet; both are thought to be original plantings.

Black Cherry
Prunus serotina
A native species found in many parts of the park, its white spring flowers are small and clustered. Birds like the tree's bitter fruit and distribute its seeds widely in their excreta. The wood is favored by makers of furniture or cabinetry; the fruit and bark are used to make cough syrup, wine and jelly. When crushed, the dark bark gives off a pungent aroma.

Flowering Cherry
Prunus serrulata
The oldest of the park's flowering cherries were presented to the park by Japan in 1912. Over the years many of these short-lived trees have succumbed to age, pollution or pests such as San Jose scale. But they are regularly replaced, and their beautiful pink and white blossoms make them popular springtime favorites. The park's many crab apple trees, which also blossom magnificently in spring, are sometimes mistaken for the smaller cherries.

London Plane
Platanus acerifolia
A hybrid of the American sycamore and the Chinese sycamore, this hardy tree was planted in the park in great numbers in the 1930s. Once hailed as a disease-resistant "super-tree," it has proved

The oldest tree in the park, believed to pre-date construction, is a London Plane adjacent to the bridle path and northeast of the Reservoir, on a parallel with 96th Street.

The Ginkgo is descended from trees that grew 150 million years ago.

susceptible to fungal attack. Yet it is sturdy and fast-growing, generally thriving in the New York climate. The smooth bark, often a mottled light tan or gray, makes it easy to identify.

Ginkgo
Ginkgo biloba

A common sight in many sections of the park, the ginkgo tree is a survivor from the age of the dinosaurs. Originally from China, imported into the West in the 18th century, the tough migrant thrives in urban streets and parks. Its distinctive leaves are, the Chinese say, "shaped like a duck's foot." In November, it drops its foul-smelling seeds, which are quickly gathered by local Asians. The nut at the center of the fruit, when roasted, is eaten as a snack or used in making soup. The nuts, or a tea made from the leaves, are said to improve memory and help women recover from childbirth.

Horse Chestnut
Aesculus hippocastanum

Originally from the Balkans, over a hundred of these trees are scattered around the park. With their spreading, rounded shape and erect clusters of springtime blossoms, they are a favorite of arborists and public alike. They are identifiable by their five-bladed leaves and thorny husks containing shiny, brown inedible nuts. The horse chestnut is not related to the American chestnut, which once was a dominant tree in the forests of the eastern United States. It fell victim to a fungus introduced from Asia in 1904 and is all but extinct, except in areas of the country where the fungus has not appeared.

American Elm
Ulmus americana

Though under attack by a deadly fungus, well over a thousand of these handsome, towering trees remain in the park and comprise one of the largest remaining stands of American elms in the country. Many are found along the Fifth Avenue boundary or lining the Mall. The Dutch elm disease, which has killed off more than half the country's American elms since the 1930s, is their mortal enemy. Only by constant inspection, pruning, and fungicide injections has the loss of these magnificent trees been held to about one percent a year. Incurably sick trees are removed, and young elms usually are planted in their place.

Black Locust
Robinia pseudoacacia

With its crusty bark and angular branching, this tree often has a somewhat Asian appearance. But it is a native tree and was one of the first New World botanical specimens shipped back to Europe around 1600. Found in many parts of the park, in June it briefly bears fragrant white blossoms. The tree was named because its fleshy black seed pods resemble the locust.

A European Beech in its full glory in late summer

The elegant span of Pine Bank Arch crosses the bridle path near Heckscher Playground on the west side of the park.

BRIDGES AND ARCHES

Wary of erecting needless structures amidst the greenery, Olmsted and Vaux included only seven small bridges in their original design for Central Park. But today thirty handsome bridges and arches, among them many recognized as architectural gems, are scattered across its landscape. How did that come about?

An unforeseen problem was partially responsible. Just as the designers had provided for sunken transverse roads to shield crosstown traffic from the park, they also planned a separation of traffic within the park. Strollers on footpaths would avoid crossing dangerous carriage driveways by using the bridges. But after construction began, park commissioners insisted on adding a bridle path, creating a third right-of-way and many more crossings. To retain the "separation of ways," more bridges and arches were needed.

Vaux, an established architect, was the man for the job. Between 1859 and 1875, he designed one span after another, often with the assistance of Jacob Wrey Mould. Their variety is dazzling, as the examples pictured here attest. Among them were seven cast-iron bridges, five of which—the Bow Bridge, the Gothic Bridge, the misnamed Pine Bank Arch and two over the bridle path on the south edge of the Reservoir—still ornament the park. Another superb example, the stone Balcony Bridge at the northwest corner of the Lake, provides an admirable view of the skyline.

Of the many arches that still survive, good examples of those built with stone, brick, or both, are the Dalehead Arch under the West Drive at 64th Street, the Willowdell Arch under the East Drive at 67th Street, the Trefoil Arch between the model boat pond and the Lake, and the Greywacke Arch under the East Drive at 80th Street.

In a far more picturesque style are such rough stone structures as the Ramble Arch in the east of that wooded area, the Riftstone Arch near Central Park West and 72nd Street, the Glen Span Arch at the south of the Loch, and the extraordinary Huddlestone Arch, a marvel of huge uncut boulders at its north.

Along with the Terrace and Belvedere Castle, the bridges and arches of the park are among Vaux's finest work in Central Park. No two are alike, since he believed that a variety of impressions are at the heart of good landscape architecture. The bridges and arches of Central Park, said Clarence Cook, the noted 19th century critic, are "not only solidly built, but as elegantly, and in as great a variety of designs, as could be contrived."

An ornamental balustrade with quatrefoil cutouts is among the features of Dalehead Arch at 64th Street, just a short distance from the Tavern on the Green.

This pathway under the rustic Glen Span Arch paralleling a narrow stream is a favorite route of bird watchers in the spring.

An engineering masterpiece, Huddlestone Arch, dating from 1866, is perhaps the most picturesque arch in the park. Designed by Calvert Vaux, it was constructed with huge uncut boulders found nearby that are held in position by gravitational forces without the use of mortar.

STATUES AND MONUMENTS

In the Mall area of the park, and scattered about its landscape or on its perimeter are dozens of statues and monuments. Some, like the Obelisk and statues of General Sherman, the heroic dog Balto, Alice in Wonderland, Hans Christian Andersen and the Angel of the Waters atop the Terrace Fountain are much admired. Others, long a part of the scenery, are often passed without a second glance.

In the early years of the park, Olmsted, Vaux and their supporters either hoped to prohibit statues, or severely limit their presence. But public pressure in favor of statuary, especially among immigrant groups, proved impossible to resist. In 1859, the German-American community donated a bust of poet Johann von Schiller, the first piece of sculpture to be erected in the park. With the floodgates open, other statuary gifts soon poured in: Alexander von Humboldt and Ludwig van Beethoven, also presented by German-Americans; Robert Burns and Walter Scott by Scottish-Americans; Thomas Moore by Irish-Americans; Guiseppe Mazzini by Italian-Americans; and Albert Thorvaldsen by Danish-Americans. In 1945, Polish-Americans celebrated the unveiling of a massive statue of Jagiello, a Medieval warrior king.

Some of the most interesting statues in the park are the work of American sculptor John Quincy Adams Ward. Beginning in the 1860s, various civic groups contributed four of his pieces including the popular *Indian Hunter* and the standing portrait of *William Shakespeare*. Other donors favored animal statuary such as *Still Hunt* and *The Falconer*, a bronze of a powerful bird poised for flight on the falconer's wrist.

In the 1920s and 1930s, the park acquired a number of light-hearted statues by Balto's sculptor, Frederick F. G. Roth, including *Dancing Bear* and *Dancing Goat*, both at the Zoo. In more recent decades the Frances Hodgson Burnett Fountain and the Untermyer Fountain were placed in the Conservatory Garden. And on the northeast corner of the park stands Central Park's newest adornment, a striking monument to jazz great Duke Ellington.

A pensive Shakespeare contemplates his own work in this piece by John Quincy Adams Ward.

The Indian Hunter *by John Quincy Adams Ward is one of the more popular works on the Mall.*

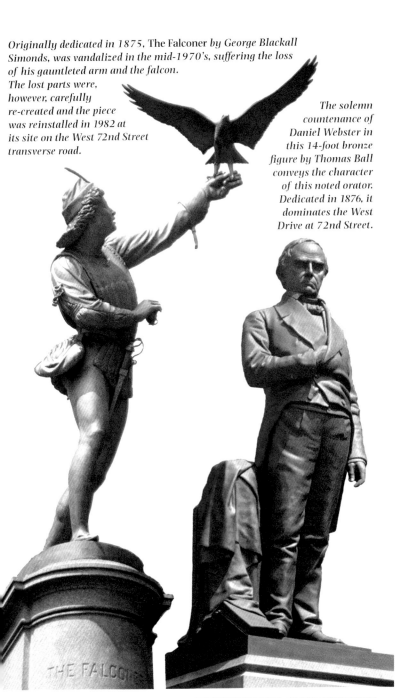

Originally dedicated in 1875, The Falconer by George Blackall Simonds, was vandalized in the mid-1970's, suffering the loss of his gauntleted arm and the falcon. The lost parts were, however, carefully re-created and the piece was reinstalled in 1982 at its site on the West 72nd Street transverse road.

The solemn countenance of Daniel Webster in this 14-foot bronze figure by Thomas Ball conveys the character of this noted orator. Dedicated in 1876, it dominates the West Drive at 72nd Street.

Crouched on a rocky outcropping along the East Drive at 76th Street, this bronze mountain lion by Edward Kemeys appears ready to spring. The artist was inspired to become a sculptor while he was a member of the team of "axmen" serving in the corps of engineers during the construction of Central Park. Rough hatch marks on the surface of Still Hunt are suggestive of a wood carver's techniques.

INDEX